Endorse

Joe shares an honest and touching tale of his journey as a bisexual recovering alcoholic—a son, husband, father and grandfather whose sobriety enabled him to make a valuable mark by helping others and building leadership in the AIDS and LGBTQ worlds.

—Lorri Jean, Retired CEO
Los Angeles LGBT Center

Joe McCormack's sweeping memoir, *Until the End is Known: A Bisexual Odyssey*, describes in exposed detail his life's journey as a bisexual during the social change of the past 50 years, and his life's work in executive searches for LGBTQ and HIV organizations that helped lead that change for our people.

What I did not know about him until reading his raw and revealingly honest memoir is that his heart is much bigger than what is visible to his clients and that his commitment to the LGBTQ and HIV community is deeply rooted in the triumphs and traumas of his personal life. But isn't that true for so many of us who find meaning and success where our heart and our expertise can be combined in open pursuits of who we are and what we hope to be? His accounting of his life shows how together they create our whole self. Joe is blessed and lucky to have so many strong memories and accomplishments that define him; and his family of origin and his wider family of choice, and surely all his clients and executive placements are the beneficiaries of all he has lived through and done.

—Jesse Milan, Jr., JD
President & CEO, AIDS United

Joe's Odyssey is shared with total honesty, allowing the reader to trust that he cherishes the truth, and that he stands tall today because he was able to embrace it. It was a privilege getting to know Joe as a bisexual Elder in recovery who gladly shares the wisdom he's discovered a step at a time.

—Brian McNaught, Author
On Being Gay and Gray

Until the End is Known
A Bisexual Odyssey

Joseph A. McCormack

Joseph A. McCormack
Palm Springs, CA

Copyright © 2024 by Joseph A. McCormack

All rights reserved.

No part of this publication may be reproduced, distributed, or transmitted in any form or by any means, including photocopying, recording, or other electronic or mechanical methods, without the prior written permission of the publisher, except as permitted by U.S. copyright law. For permission requests, contact the publisher.

For privacy reasons, some names, locations, and dates may have been changed.

First paperback edition July 2024

Book design by AquaZebra.com

AquaZebra™
Web, Book & Print Design

Library of Congress Control Number: 2024911102

ISBN: 979-8-218-38260-5 (paperback)

Published by Joseph A. McCormack

1074 E San Lucas Rd
Palm Springs, CA 92264

joemccormack1214@gmail.com

Dedication

This memoir is dedicated to my husband Gary, whose proofreading and commentary have helped me become a better writer, to Glen Vecchione, who empowered me to transform journalism into storytelling, and to Stephen Sturk, whose meticulous editing has resulted in a better final document.

Table of Contents

Introduction ix
Chapter 1   The Past & Future Disappear....................1
Chapter 2   Cherry Picking... 3
Chapter 3   A Meritocracy of Nerds 9
Chapter 4   Wrestling with a Problem............................17
Chapter 5   Jesuits & Banjo Sing-Alongs.......................21
Chapter 6   A Tragedy or a Statistic?............................. 25
Chapter 7   I Leave the Valley of Heart's Delight 29
Chapter 8   The Budget Socialite 35
Chapter 9   Taking a Bite of the Big Apple 41
Chapter 10   If You Can Make It There,
             You'll Make It Anywhere. 45
Chapter 11   It's Not Just a Job. It's an Adventure. 51
Chapter 12   My Missing Irish Cousin...............................61
Chapter 13   The Return of the Native 65
Chapter 14   The Priceless Table 71
Chapter 15   The Turning Point..75
Chapter 16   Four Thousand Entrepreneurs......................... 79
Chapter 17   Cooking for James Beard 83
Chapter 18   The Journey of 12 Steps Begins in a Basement..89
Chapter 19   If Opportunity Doesn't Knock, Build a Door ...97
Chapter 20   Recruiting the Perfect Candidate 101
Chapter 21   Captured by French Vogue 105
Chapter 22   And Baby Makes Three................................107

Chapter 23	My Best Man	111
Chapter 24	The City of Sunshine & Flowers	115
Chapter 25	The Children Serve Us Spaghetti	119
Chapter 26	Count No Man Happy	123
Chapter 27	In the Middle of Life's Journey	129
Chapter 28	Talking to Earthquakes	133
Chapter 29	Almost Under the Hollywood Sign	137
Chapter 30	The Viennese Collector	139
Chapter 31	Professional Growing Pains	145
Chapter 32	Loyalty & Betrayal	151
Chapter 33	Red Devil Tools Fights AIDS	157
Chapter 34	Icarus Takes Off from Kurdistan	159
Chapter 35	A Very Good Life	165
Chapter 36	Success in Public & Trouble in the Family	171
Chapter 37	Two Mothers & Two Fathers	175
Chapter 38	What's the Point?	181
Chapter 39	The First Time I Retired	185
Chapter 40	Darshans & Dish Towels	191
Chapter 41	Ashes to Ashes	197
Chapter 42	Ashes to Ashes, Part 2	201
Chapter 43	My Life Until Now	205
Chapter 44	What I Have Lived For	209
Epilogue		213
About the Author		215

Until the End is Known
A Bisexual Odyssey

Introduction

I've been blessed with an extraordinary life and a fulfilling one. I've witnessed more than half of the 20th century and two decades of the 21st, both eventful eras. I've played a modest role in addressing the AIDS epidemic and advancing gay liberation. I've done my best to be a good father, grandfather, husband, and friend. I've had the privilege of mentoring a few extraordinary young men and women who've gone on to success as judges, physicians, creative artists, and business executives. I have sponsored people in 12-step programs whose lives changed for the better as when they realized, in sobriety, their full potential. If I have a legacy, I hope it's this: I've guided others along their paths, just as my mentors and sponsors guided me.

Am I merely the protagonist of my life, predetermined by circumstances, or am I the author of my story? I suspect it's a combination. I haven't always made the best choices, but my choices have been healthier as I've grown in experience and wisdom. And I write my story because I hope it will interest my grandchildren—this account of my nearly 80 years on this planet. All events are portrayed from my point of view, and I realize that others may have experienced them differently.

Some of the names and places herein have been changed, composite characters portrayed as one, and dialogue reconstructed when no clear memory remains. In keeping with the tradition of anonymity, living AA members have been identified by their first name and the first initial of their last name only. I have tried to stay true to the authenticity of my experience as I remember it.

Chapter 1

The Past & Future Disappear

"Every moment that changes your life changes who you are."
—Anonymous

I don't remember the crash.

I feel the sensation of the car spinning, hear muffled shouting, then I wake up on the tarmac surrounded by police and paramedics. When I turn my head and look between them, I see the remains of my car folded into a "V" shape, windshield pulverized, passenger doors dangling, the whole mess of it smoking beside a twisted stanchion. Johnny cries out in pain as they lift him on a stretcher, but thank God, he's alive. Tim is surrounded by the urgent ministrations of paramedics and no sound comes out of him. I try to speak, but a searing pain in my knee and the stinging in my eye that I take to be blood, keeps me from saying much of anything. I'd decided to drive us home after our night out in the gay bars of San Francisco. I recall the winding road, my vision blurring, and sleepiness overtaking me.

***

I dream of late summer, the sun low on the field, the weedy yard of a ramshackle packing plant. The smell of cherries, bruised cherries— mounds of them, mildly fermented, but still deliciously sweet. My best friends, Artie and Ronnie and I laugh as we gather and gather in our buckets. Cherry gathering! To take home for mom's cobblers after supper, the scent of flour on her apron. I race back, faster than usual, but just as I step on the porch of our house, something happens: a bang, a smash, an earthquake? —something bad!

I come to as I am being lifted by the paramedics into an ambulance.

The next morning, I wake up in a Stanford University Hospital room when Johnny appears at my bedside in a wheelchair.

"How's Tim?" I ask.

Johnny hesitates, looks down at the floor, "Tim died last night."

Chapter 2
Cherry Picking

*"Cherry trees will blossom every year,
but I'll disappear for good one of these days."*
–Phillip Whalen

A cherry-packing plant stood between our newly purchased house in East San Jose and the elementary school. Each day, the packers would arrive to sort out the imperfect or damaged cherries and dump them in a large pile behind the plant. The plant and others like it, more rickety sheds than sturdy factories, were a familiar sight throughout the rural Santa Clara Valley long before the tech revolution.

So, in the quiet of San Jose summer evenings, after the packers finished their work and drove off, the shed stood forlorn and unguarded, inviting us to raid and plunder. Our reward: scores of sweet, if slightly bruised, cherries and sticky desserts until the first chill of autumn. I don't remember how we discovered this, but my friends and I would arrive after the plant closed and return home with scores of cherries, many with only slight imperfections.

My cherry-gathering friends, Artie and Ronnie, lived next door. Both my age with two younger brothers. They were the product of a blended family and got along well. If they fought, it never became obvious, unlike the shouting matches at our house. Quiet and introspective, there was something vulnerable, but very appealing about Artie, so unlike his rambunctious brothers.

Down the block lived Tommy, who was a head taller than us, though the same age. Farther down Virginia Place, Herbie.

We spent hours outdoors in the spring, summer and fall playing Kick the Can, Hide and Seek and, later, softball in an empty and dusty lot on the corner. We were a gang from about 6 to 10 years of age. Our parents never worried about us so long as we came home for dinner. We had a dog named Rusty who was let loose to play in the morning, and he always came home for dinner as well. It was a more innocent time for boys and dogs.

My neighbors and pals Artie on the left and Ronnie on the right, with my dog Rusty, San Jose 1952

My mother and father, Joe & Cecelia McCormack, circa 1943

My mother Cecelia, my older sister Elizabeth and I had arrived in San Jose, then known as the "Valley of Heart's Delight," a year earlier following the sudden death from heart failure of my father in New York. Born at the Boulevard Hospital in Astoria, one subway-stop from Queens to Manhattan via the 59th Street Bridge, I lived my first four years in a two-bedroom New York apartment just a block away from Astoria Boulevard, the main commercial street in the area.

My father worked at various jobs in the city, which included being a waiter at Child's Restaurant, one of the country's first restaurant chains, and as an elevator operator in a residential building on West 77th Street, where my mother worked as a nanny for a New York City detective and his family. I imagine there were a lot of ups and downs in their relationship.

On a snowy Christmas Eve in 1942, Joe and Cecelia went to see *Gone with the Wind;* after dinner at Child's Restaurant, he asked, "Will you marry me?" And so began my history.

For breakfast, my father loved soft-boiled eggs, and I learned to love them too. I remember jumping up into his arms when he came through the front door after work and going to the park with him on weekends.

My mother had a complex, long-distance relationship with my older sister Elizabeth. She had been born in Austria, a result (I was to hear from my mother's sister Caroline) of a sexual assault by a soldier who had been passing through the village near the Hungarian border where she lived. This was an intensely painful memory for my mother, who couldn't speak of it without tears. My mother arrived in this country with only one gift from her family—two of the finest eiderdown comforters with cotton covers. She never used them herself, but they kept my sister and me warm on the coldest nights.

My father agreed to adopt Elizabeth when he married my mother.

"Let's hire an attorney and bring her to New York," he offered.

Elizabeth and I got along well in those early years. When she was old enough for high school, I was the annoying little brother who did my best to embarrass her. We shared a room with twin beds.

"She shakes her bed and moans at night," I complained to anyone who would listen.

I was to learn years later, before my first trip to Ireland, that my father had a sister named Margaret who had also had an illegitimate child. In the church-dominated Ireland of those days, she was undoubtedly forced to give up the child for adoption, and she never married. Perhaps that's why my father felt some compassion for my mother and Elizabeth.

My father's early death in New York was to leave a hole in my psyche that I spent a good part of my early life trying to fill. Not long after, my mother's sister Caroline invited us to join her in California.

We spent that first year living with my aunt and her husband, who had purchased a restaurant near a truck route into South San Jose from the Bayshore Freeway. The restaurant, a drive-in with teenage carhops, provided employment as an inside waitress for my more mature mother, who had two children to feed. It also supplied me with free milkshakes, which enabled me to play the generous host for my friends until my uncle cut off my credit.

Besides my immediate family and the second family of my aunt and uncle, I soon found another family, the DeLucas. Mr. and Mrs. DeLuca were first generation Sicilians and lived with their sprawling family in a house close-by. They were to play an important role in my later life after we moved across town to Virginia Place, where I went to work as a teenager in their grocery store. Their oldest son was named Kelly, not a common Sicilian name. Kelly DeLuca would one day sign my paychecks.

My mother was attractive, warm, and loving, with an Austrian accent that only added to her charm. Still a young woman, it wasn't surprising that she longed for another relationship, which she soon found with Chester, a cook in the restaurant. Tall, with dark wavy hair and an Errol Flynn mustache, he wooed her until she accepted his marriage proposal.

She was warned by co-workers: "You know he drinks a lot, right?"

Like my father, Chester had had rheumatic fever, which disqualified him for military service. Also, like my father, he assuredly had a problem with alcohol. My father was a periodic drinker who occasionally went on a bender. Between sprees, he was a responsible parent and husband.

Chester was a daily drinker who was seldom completely sober. He spent World War II in the Civilian Conservation Corps, where he learned how to cook. One of the few amusing memories I have of him is calling someone a cock sucker, a term I had never heard before.

Picturing a male hummingbird, I asked him, "Is that like the birds who fly around flowers?"

Looking embarrassed and flustered, he was unwilling to offer a definition.

No doubt my mother felt that all he needed was a good woman to straighten him out, a sentiment echoed by thousands of women in recovery from co-dependence. As you might expect, she was not able to fix his alcohol problem, although his cooking steadily improved. Medical authorities debate whether alcoholism is genetic. I was to find out many years later when alcohol became a problem in my life.

Moving across town opened a world of new adventures.

Chapter 3

A Meritocracy of Nerds

"Be nice to nerds. You may end up working for them."
–Charles J. Sykes

Our new family moved to Virginia Place in East San Jose, the first house my parents owned. It was a white, two-bedroom, single-bath house on a corner lot, surrounded by a picket fence.

I enrolled in a new elementary school, and my new friends became that version of "Our Gang," harvesting the summer cherries. Our neighborhood was one of those post-war developments in San Jose, built on what had previously been a dairy farm. The realtor promised us that a city bus route would be established to the neighborhood soon, a promise that was never fulfilled. For years, we had to walk a mile north, past the occasional cow, to the nearest bus stop. We were too poor to own a car, so we got plenty of exercise walking. We had a Chevy for a couple of months, but it disappeared one day, hauled away by a tow truck.

My mother had two more children with my stepfather: Steven and Marianne. My brother Steven probably suffers from Level 3 autism, although the condition was unnamed at the time. He was labeled severely retarded. As he didn't attend school, I was often called to babysit when my parents were out.

My younger sister Marianne became my closest sibling and an important part of my life. As I was nearly nine years older, I think I played more of a paternal role for her after my stepfather's death. I introduced her to books I liked, such as *Gulliver's Travels* and *Alice's Adventures in Wonderland*, and I may have inspired a love for learning in her that led to a college and a teaching career.

"Study something you love," I advised. "Don't worry about preparing for a job."

When she decided to major in biology in college, I could be of little help.

"I don't know beans about botany," I wrote.

I see the best of our mother in Marianne. She rarely says an unkind word about anyone, and I know no one who dislikes her.

Autistic children have difficulty establishing relationships. Our mother was devoted to Steven until her death, but it would be disingenuous to say that Marianne or I had any semblance of a normal relationship with him. It was always slightly embarrassing to have friends over for the first time to have to explain Steven's condition, as he had free reign of the house. Until my mother's death, he lived with her. Later, we found a group home where he was and is cared for.

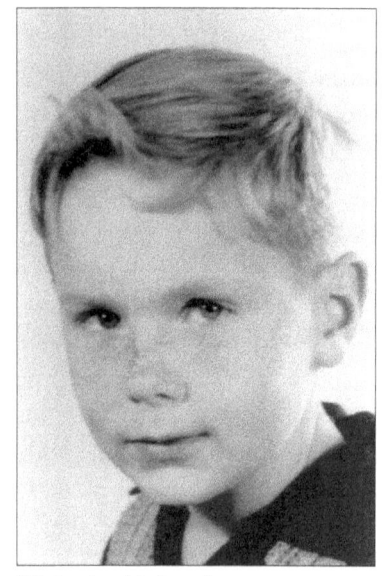

***

Me in the third grade at 8 years old, 1953

At eight years old, I joined the Cub Scouts, supervised by a den mother who mainly taught us arts and crafts. On a typical after school visit, I'd be elbow deep in scraps of colored paper and library paste or making yet another multicolored lanyard with plastic strips at her kitchen table. Our supreme achievement was the creation of a coffee table-size clay ash tray that was kiln-fired and presented solemnly to our parents.

Later I graduated to the Boy Scouts and the Explorers

and camping trips in the Santa Cruz Mountains and in the High Sierras. Two-man pup tents offered opportunities for sexual exploration for adolescent boys still too awkward to talk to girls. Once a year we would travel as a group to Strawberry Lake in the Gold Country, where there was an old vacation lodge, as well as surrounding campgrounds. I remember the pine scent as we drove up into the mountains, the smell of our campfires as we cooked breakfast and the lazy warm summer days, hiking and swimming in the cold mountain lake to earn our merit badges. *Volare* was on the hit parade then, and it will always remind me of our car ride to camp.

At 10 years old, I discovered the public library downtown. I would regularly walk to the mile-distant city bus stop, deposit my token and take the 20-minute ride to the old Romanesque San Jose Central Library. There I discovered science fiction, and I became an avid reader of Isaac Asimov, Ray Bradbury and Arthur C. Clarke.

Downtown San Jose had a handful of commercial streets in the 1950s. Businesses were located on First Street or Santa Clara Street. At the intersection of the two were the Bank of America, the tallest building in town, and our two local independent department stores: Hart's and Roos Brothers across from one another. On First Street were three movie theaters where I could see a first run film for 25 cents. *Original Joe's* restaurant down the block served the best hamburgers in town, presented on a garlic roll with crisp french fries, fresh from the fryer.

My books and I often awaited the bus for home in front of Carrol & Bishop, a soda fountain and news stand, where I could leaf through the comic books and magazines at no charge.

"Hey, kid, are you gonna buy anything?" asked the soda jerk.

"Just looking," I'd reply, returning the now dog-eared comic books to the rack.

On a typical Saturday I would be struggling with my chin-high stack of books up the one-mile hike to our house, wishing that someone would invent a book bag.

Across the street from our Virginia Place house was the White Tiger Market, a neighborhood grocery store, common long before the big supermarket chains. It was owned by the very same DeLuca family who lived across the street from my aunt and uncle in the old neighborhood. When I'd shop for my mother, they offered at no charge to count the freckles I'd sprouted.

"Hold still," Kelly DeLuca would say. "We're almost done."

I often returned home with a black beard and mustache, looking like a junior version of Guy Fawkes, along with the groceries and an approximate freckle count.

I was becoming an adolescent, and on one of our camping trips I had my first cigarette, a Newport menthol smoke as I recall, which started a tobacco habit that I didn't give up until 15 years later. On another of our camping trips to the Big Sur on a rainy weekend, I left home as tenor and returned as a baritone, which surprised everyone in my family. My sister Elizabeth offered me cough drops.

"Sounds like you caught a bad cold," she said.

***

My best friend in the Scouts was Wayne Higashi. His father had served in the U.S. Army and his mother was a native-born Japanese. His father joined the Army during World War II to get his family out of the internment camps. They had me over for my first dinner of sukiyaki. I thought it was terribly exotic at the time. Wayne developed hepatitis when we were about nine years old, and he became a shut-in for several months. I visited him, biking half-mile north of us on King Road, several times a week, and we formed a friendship that would last for 70 years. Wayne and I were to cross paths again and again in our adult lives, long after the "Valley of Heart's Delight" became Silicon Valley, and the orchards, packing sheds and farms were only a memory.

While Wayne quarantined at home for several weeks, I brought him the work from school he was missing. Up through middle school, we continued to be the best of friends. We went through the Cub Scouts, Boy Scouts and Explorers together and spent a couple of summers away at camp in the High Sierras at Strawberry Lake.

Mayfair Elementary School was about three long blocks from our house, and I walked to and from school daily. Off campus religious instruction was a weekly feature in the California public schools of that era. As a nominal Catholic, I opted to go to Friday morning Catechism in a Quonset hut with wooden benches where two fierce-looking nuns in the full black habits of their order supervised our memorization of the tenets of the church. I had no deep-seated religious convictions except to please Sister Calasanctius, who sported a faint mustache, and who seemed ever ready with a ruler to discipline those who couldn't offer the correct response to questions like, "Why did God make me?"

Mayfair Elementary School Musicians 1955. I'm on the drums.

Another good friend was Scotty Pricer, and we became the co-captains of the Safety Patrol, serving as crossing-guards for the younger kids when school was let out. Scotty was blond and handsome, and I was attracted to him in a way that pre-dated my sexual awareness. This leadership role of immense importance was my first clue that I was destined for greatness. I also played the drums (badly) as part of our school band. When I was in the sixth grade, I was encouraged by my teacher to try out for the Christmas pageant, where I played King Herod, with a crepe wool beard and as much malice and villainy as I could muster. I'm sure I could do a better job today.

Often it was dusk or dark in the winter months after band practice or theater rehearsal when I walked home from school. San Jose has a Mediterranean climate, but winter nights got cold enough to see your breath and frost to form on the lawn. While walking I would look up at the stars in a crystal-clear sky and dream about the future, which always involved leaving San Jose and moving to some exciting big city. I was in search of something larger and more meaningful than our small-town life, and it wasn't an answer I found in Catechism. It was to be the quest of my lifetime.

When I entered the seventh grade, I was bused to Pala Junior High on the upper east side of the valley. Returning home from school one day, I heard that my stepfather Chester had had a massive heart attack. Suddenly, he was gone from our lives, just like my father had been.

I had done well in elementary school and was tested for advanced placement, so I was assigned an algebra tutor and placed in a Montessori-like class called the "Workshop," where we were encouraged to follow our own interests in addition to pursuing some of the core curriculum. Seventh and eighth grade adolescents in my experience are clannish, judgmental, and cruel. Being in a gifted class immediately marked me as "a brain." I wasn't very good at sports, so outside my immediate class I was largely ostracized. It didn't help that I insisted on getting a flat-top, badly executed by my reluctant barber and resembling nothing so much as a double mullet on either side of my head. If there are any pictures of me at that age, it's only because I haven't yet burned them.

One of our classmates was a girl named Meredith, who had reached puberty early enough to sport (to us) enormous breasts, apparent with her close-fitting sweaters. We all had fantasies about Meredith. She was friendly enough, but totally unconscious of her sex appeal. Meredith was surrounded by 12- and 13-year-old boys with erections, an innocent maiden surrounded by unicorns, but she was focused on solving square root problems and building her science project. I was too nervous to talk to her, let alone kiss her.

***

In 1959, our middle school class split off into three high schools, including the long-established James Lick High School and the two newly established campuses of Samuel Ayer and Andrew Hill, built to serve San Jose's growing population. Wayne went east to Samuel Ayer, and I went south to Andrew Hill.

I got my first job as a bag boy in the De Lucas' neighborhood grocery, and I was to work there all through high school. One day a new produce man named Fred Kelly showed up. He had just been released from prison. I finally mustered up the courage to ask why he'd been in the lockup.

"Income tax evasion," he replied.

He must have made a lot of money from eggplant and melons, I thought.

I continued to visit Wayne, now living on the east side of the valley, from time to time. Through him, I met the Murdock Family, including their beautiful daughter Rose, whom I invited to my senior prom. Wayne and Rose enrolled at San Jose State College after high school, and I enrolled at the University of Santa Clara—and later at Berkeley. So, as sometimes happens, life flowed between us, as we took different forks in the river.

These were my roots, my family and friends—those whom I'd lose and others who remain close to me today as I continue my journey.

Things were about to take a dramatic change as I left middle school for the new high school closer to my home, which had just enrolled its first graduating class. I decided I needed a better version of myself for my new school.

Chapter 4
Wrestling with a Problem

"Be yourself; everyone else is already taken."
–Oscar Wilde

A fresh start at a new high school meant leaving behind my friends at Pala Junior High, but it allowed me to re-invent myself. I started off in sophomore geometry rather than Algebra 1 which already marked me as smart—a dubious friend-making advantage in those days and almost certainly an invitation to get bullied. So, by my sophomore year, I knew that playing sports and running for class government became essential tools for survival. Soon (and probably to everyone's surprise) I became sophomore class president and joined the football, wrestling and track teams.

I didn't excel in football, and it didn't help that our coach, blowing his whistle and brandishing his clip board, thought that explosive eruptions improved performance and built a good team. Some players responded to his brand of coaching. I did not. He was my first lesson in bad leadership, a lesson I quickly absorbed.

My wrestling coach, however, was a man deeply respected by his team. Small and wiry, he was both tough and compassionate. If he asked us to run five miles, he would lead the group. A blackbelt judo master, he exemplified patience and preparation. He brought out the best in us by working one on one with each wrestler and by offering praise and encouragement when he saw improvement. I won more matches than I lost. The wrestling coach was my second leadership experience and one who taught me the value of leading by example, as well as of offering individual attention and praise.

I enjoyed wrestling because it provided close body contact with another young man. Now I realize that I was experiencing the early stirrings of homoerotic feelings. Regardless of who won or lost, we were nearly always on friendly terms. I was fair-haired and blue eyed, and my exercise routine, which included weightlifting, had given me a muscular build. One day, Penny Kennedy visited the wrestling room after practice, where we were in typical wrestler's skin-tight singlets. She must have liked what she saw because she later agreed to go with me to my first school dance.

Track was merely a spring exercise in fitness. Short and stocky, I had the right build for wrestling and absolutely the wrong build for track. I had to run the 1320 (three laps around a quarter mile track), followed by throwing the shotput, which I could hardly pick up after an exhausting race. Years later, running indoors at the New York Athletic Club, I shared the track with Irish distance runner and Olympian Eamonn Coghlan who ran two laps to my one. I noticed that he had four-foot-long legs and a light upper torso, the perfect build for his sport.

Now 15 years old, I discovered that alcohol did for me what it does for many problem drinkers—it gave me self-confidence and as AA founder Bill Wilson said, "I fancied myself a leader. The drive for success was on." Drinking was a weekend thing in high school, more beer than anything else. Like in the film *American Graffiti*, our usual weekend activity was "cruising the main," driving our cars up and down the two main streets in San Jose, with occasional stops at a pizza parlor or a drive-in restaurant like Mel's Drive-In or the Holland Creamery. I had a fake ID, easy enough to do with the early copy machines and the paper draft cards many carried. Or an older friend would just buy liquor for us.

Richard, one of our high school friends, had a cabin in Santa Cruz, across the coastal mountain range from San Jose. It belonged to his family, and we were not supposed to use it without permission, but Richard knew where there was a hidden key. My best high school friend Jimmy and I and several of our friends drove over the mountain to spend time at the beach and to drink—but mainly to drink. Working at the grocery store, I had fellow cashier friends who were old enough to buy liquor, so I was the designated supplier for the weekend. We concocted a disgusting punch made of vodka, sloe gin and brandy, and it was the first time I can remember getting rip roaring drunk, but it wouldn't be the last.

After a night of hard partying, Jimmy and I shared a bed, and I soon discovered he had some things to teach me. I had never French kissed a man before. In fact, I had never French kissed anyone.

The next day ("Boy, were we drunk last night!"), we played touch football on the beach, which is jarring with a hangover, but I was happy to hang with this group of close male friends—and a soon-to-be occasional bed-partner Jimmy.

In the 1960s there was no possibility of "coming out" if you didn't want to be an outcast, so we both dated girls and often went on double dates, but we talked every day about everything except our sexual attraction for each other and were inseparable. My first high school date with a girl was with Penny Kennedy, the wrestling fan, whom I took to the sophomore dance. She must have found me very boring when I wasn't in wrestling tights because she went home with someone else. I later dated girls from other high schools, including a girl from a Catholic School who introduced me to the nuns when I picked her up. She didn't expect me to get sexual with her, and the nuns, who reminded me of my catechism teachers, terrified me in any case. They formed a panel that approved the girls' escorts, and I had the suspicion that they harbored weaponized rulers under their habits.

"You look like a nice young man—and a Catholic too, I hear," said one. As a male virgin, I guess I passed muster.

In my junior year, I was selected by my high school to attend Boys' State in Sacramento. Sponsored by the American Legion, Boys' State is an opportunity for youngsters who've shown leadership potential to learn about state government while camped out on cots at the cavernous convention center in the state capital. It was one of my first experiences rubbing shoulders with an elite, high potential group of fellow high school leaders, and it was an exciting—and also homoerotic—experience. Somewhere there is a photo of us posed at the Capitol in 1964, and I will always fondly remember the experience and the friends I made.

Senior year I was again elected class president, and I began applying to regional schools that would offer me a scholarship. There was no college fund set aside for my education. My mother, now a widow, had to work two jobs to put food on the table for the three children at home. I sometimes wonder whether I could have gotten into an Ivy League school with my grades and SAT scores, but it seemed so far out of the realm of financial possibility that I never gave it serious thought as a teenager. But acceptance to college was in my future, and ultimately my ticket out of San Jose.

Chapter 5
Jesuits & Banjo Sing-Alongs

"We are all butterflies, Earth is our chrysalis."
—LeeAnn Taylor

Built in the Spanish revival style around an early California Mission, the University of Santa Clara campus was spread over 106 lush acres of palm trees and native California flowers and plants. Compared to nearby San Jose State University, the 120-year-old institution had an intimate feel and a unified culture of scholarship and learning encouraged by the Jesuits.

I was selected for an Honors Tutorial Program for gifted students, based upon the Great Books, a 54-book set published by Encyclopedia Britannica, representing, in the editors' opinion, the Western canon of important thought. I was offered full tuition and early acceptance.

The summer reading list before my freshman year included over a dozen books, including *The Idea of a University* by John Cardinal Newman, Alexis de Tocqueville's *Democracy in America*, Plato's *Republic*—and other light reading. I learned from *The Idea of a University* that a liberal arts education does not train a person for a specific job or career. It's intended to teach one to reason, to think critically and to develop an intellectual curiosity. I soon discovered that high school, which had been such a breeze for me, did not adequately prepare me for the academic rigor and extensive reading required by a Jesuit college, where most of the students had been prepared by a Catholic prep school.

However, I have always loved learning and found that the courses of greatest interest to me were theology and philosophy, attempts by generations of writers to understand life's great questions. Far from indoctrinating me in Catholicism after a childhood's passing acquaintance, courses like the Religious History of Israel gave me the historical context to understand the development of monotheism and the Old Testament. It took a while to get up to speed on philosophy. Aristotle and Thomas Aquinas are not light reading, but it was helpful to understand their historical context and their influences on modern thought. I especially enjoyed Aristotle's *Metaphysics*, which skillfully demonstrates the existence of God through logic. It left me still unconvinced emotionally.

The Honors Program was directed by former University of Chicago professor Harold Knox, who, along with his male companion Peter, moved to Santa Clara for the position. He lent gravitas to the new program and a bit of intrigue since we all suspected that Dr. Knox and Peter were a couple. But nobody spoke openly about it in those days. It was my first example of a committed, long-term gay relationship and a powerful illustration to me of possibilities later in life.

Each of us was assigned a tutor. Unfortunately, my tutor was neither kind nor scholarly. We took an immediate dislike to each other. Marnie Merkin had the pinched manner of a spinster, perpetually disappointed at her lot in life, with a joyless approach to teaching. I could sense her irritation at my superficial preparation, and there was mutual hostility whenever we met.

"How much of the commentary on Plato's *Republic* have you read," she'd ask.

"Well, some of it," I replied, to her obvious displeasure and ready grimace. As in sports, I respond better to encouragement than criticism in learning, and we were simply mismatched.

Once I started college, drinking became more frequent. There was—and still is—a culture of binge drinking on campuses everywhere. If you want to be a cool kid and fit in, it's almost a requirement. And it wasn't discouraged by the Jesuits, who had few other sanctioned corporal pleasures.

My sophomore year, several important events occurred. I took a course that introduced me to sociology and cultural relativity. I was relieved to learn that sexual mores were a construct particular to our culture—and sometimes baffling to other cultures. As my semester project, I decided to explore the homosexual subculture in San Francisco, which I had discovered quite by accident when my high school friend Jimmy and I were at a beatnik party in a loft in North Beach one night. Neither of us knew that there were many like us attracted to other men, and it was an exciting discovery for both of us. I was elated to discover a whole new world that would open for me.

I was soon frequenting the bars (with a fake ID) and the after-hours clubs like the Last Resort, the Black Cat Café with José Sarria and the Gilded Cage with Charles Pierce, two of the famous female impersonators of their day. The Embarcadero YMCA, celebrated years later by the Village People, was a famous meeting place for sailors, college students and middle-aged married men in the city. I got an A on my semester sociology paper, which encouraged me to do more research.

San Jose, a small, provincial town in those days, had its own secret gay population. The publisher of a local newspaper and the owner of one of the city's two independent downtown department stores were part of a coterie of prominent local gay citizens who socialized with each other.

At the other end of the spectrum was The Crystal Palace, San Jose's only gay bar, shared at the time by local lesbians who monopolized the pool table.

"Anyone want play a game of eight ball?" I asked.

"This table is for women only," replied a big woman with a tank top, a cross neck tattoo and a buzz cut. "Go back up front with the sissies where you belong."

I decided then and there that I wanted to be part of the more upscale crowd—professionals and college students like me.

About this time, I had started meeting gay students from Berkeley, Stanford, San Jose State and other surrounding colleges, and we would caravan to San Francisco to party on weekends. The most popular bar for the college crowd was the Rendezvous on Sutter Street, discreetly located above a wedding photographer. Sundays offered 25-cent draft beer and banjo sing-along nights, and we rarely missed one. Unfortunately, my fascination with the subculture was not conducive to rigorous scholarship, and my GPA had fallen below the 3.75 required to remain in the Honors Program.

There were more adventures in store for me, not all of them happy ones.

Chapter 6

A Tragedy or a Statistic?

*"Once you've consumed your first drink,
you've lost that ability to make a sound judgment."
–MADD Chapter President Penny Wagner*

"Tim died last night, Johnny?" I repeat without believing it.

Johnny gives the left wheel of his wheelchair a quarter-turn to face the window.

"The paramedics couldn't save him. He died right there in the road."

I look out the window of Stanford University Hospital at the sun-dappled lawn and shade trees the morning after the accident. I'm aware of the distant squeak of a gurney, a muffled cough from down the hall, a monitor beeping nearby, the soft tread of unseen nurses—a symphony of hushed anxieties. Rather than grief or shock, I feel only numbness, probably a form of disassociation to protect myself from the full impact of my responsibility as the driver of the car. Other feelings—of grief and remorse—would come later.

By 1970, there were 25,000 drunk driving deaths in the United States. Tim was one of them. This is the story of his death, reflected upon after nearly 60 years by the adult I have now become.

We three—myself, Tim Acheson and Johnny Sykes—good college chums, left the Rendezvous Bar on Sutter Street at 2 am. We're drinking heavily with fake IDs—cheap whiskey—and I'm wondering if I should be concerned that one drink follows another so easily until keeping count doesn't matter anymore. Because I'm young and with my friends and enjoying life.

I had no business driving home that night with my two passengers. I could hold a lot of liquor without showing any obvious signs that I was drunk. I underestimated how seriously it affected my judgment. It wasn't the first time I had made that 50-mile drive back to the Santa Clara Valley after a night in San Francisco. I had done it several times in a blackout, losing track of the entire trip until I found myself pulling up to my garage door. I didn't think there was anything abnormal about that.

My car, which had veered off the Bayshore Freeway, had hit a steel directional sign column.

Johnny wound up with a badly broken arm and other injuries. I have broken a bone near my kneecap and a laceration that required stitches above my right eye. I was in the driver's seat, but the passenger side of the car had hit the stanchion, so they received the major force of the impact. I was grateful to be sedated and put into an ambulance.

***

After a couple of days, I was released from the hospital. The night I came home I knew I had to call Tim's parents to explain what had happened. I don't remember what I said, but we talked for quite a while. It was sincere and emotional for all of us. Although I am weeping, sitting on a single bed in my boyhood bedroom, I feel oddly disembodied during our conversation, as though I am watching myself perform an important but painful duty.

One day, as I was under a shade tree reading the Bible for one of my courses, the brother of the boy who was killed came to see me. I suspected that he wanted to see if we were affluent enough to satisfy a judgment from a lawsuit for damages. I think one look at our modest two-bedroom house with a broken screen door and me in a cast reading the Bible persuaded him it would be a lost cause. However, meeting with him enabled me to make amends again, such as they were, in person.

I gave the money I had from insurance to Johnny for his medical expenses. The only positive outcome of the accident is that it diverted me from the downward spiral of my trajectory, which was not headed toward any happy ending. I often tell people that had the accident happened today, I would probably be serving time for manslaughter. There were no strict drunk driving laws or seatbelts in those pre-MADD days.

Immobilized, with my left leg in a cast, I had plenty of time to study and bring my grades up, which were beginning to suffer after my discovery of the gay scene. In that pre-Stonewall era, gay social life was almost exclusively to be found in gay bars, typically run by organized crime who paid the police off to prevent harassment. I also had plenty of time to think about the direction my life was taking and whether I wanted to stay at the University of Santa Clara, even though I was on full scholarship.

When I had recovered enough to be mobile, I discovered that the Greyhound Bus made several trips a night to and from San Francisco. Starved for fellowship, I began taking the bus, trying to drink more moderately or not at all, and I left the driving to a professional.

Over the next few months, I pulled my grades up, but I was ready for a change, and that's when I met Jeff.

Chapter 7
I Leave the Valley of Heart's Delight

"You can't go home again because home has ceased to exist except in the mothballs of memory."
–John Steinbeck

Freed from my leg cast, I began a more cautious approach to gay nightlife, taking the bus to San Francisco and frequenting the after-hours places where there was no alcohol. One night at a club called the Last Resort near the Embarcadero YMCA, I met Jeff Lowell, and he fit my type: "preppy" in khakis and a blue button-down shirt with neatly trimmed chestnut hair and a swimmer's build. He looked like a contemporary ad from a J. Crew catalogue. After making eye contact, Jeff followed me into the restroom where I was combing my hair.

"Hi, my name is Jeff." he said. "What are you doing later?"

"Well, I don't have a car," I replied, so I'm staying next door at the Embarcadero Y."

The Embarcadero Y was a handy and inexpensive place to spend the night in the city. It was notorious for the hanky-panky in the communal showers and for the doors ajar at many of the rooms.

"Why don't you drive with us to Palo Alto?" suggested Jeff. "I'm staying with a friend at Stanford."

"Sounds great", said I, "But how will I get home tomorrow?"

"Don't worry," he said with a smile. "We'll make sure you're delivered home safely."

Now on the cusp of adulthood at 19, I was ready for something more than a one-night stand. Jeff was to become my first real boyfriend and a reason to transfer to UC Berkeley, where I was to spend the next three years.

Our Palo Alto host David was a Stanford graduate student, who was affectionately referred to as "Mother" by the odd collection of gay college students who assembled at his three-bedroom tract house, a mile from campus, on a regular basis, mostly Berkeley and Stanford kids. This familial arrangement, presided over by a slightly older gay man, was common in the 1960s. Each of us was given a "camp" name, and I was Patty McCormack, named after the evil young actress in *The Bad Seed*. It's ironic that my future wife was to bear that name many years later.

Cross-dressing and flamboyance were accepted behavior in private, probably because it was a protest against prevailing gender stereotypes as well as a pastime in gay circles. We did a lot of drinking, and I smoked my first marijuana cigarette at one of David's frequent parties. A Stanford senior, who was to become my roommate a couple of years later in Berkeley, drove me home after my first weekend at David's.

Jeff was terrific sex, but he also loved to drink and could be relentlessly negative and critical. Curiously, he had the same birthday as I did, but he was two years older, so he graduated earlier than I from Cal. Jeff went directly into the Peace Corps with a degree in Comparative Literature, and he was sent to Malawi to teach math and science to the local youth. There wasn't a big demand for Latin and French classics in Central Africa at the time.

My first love, Jeff Lowell 1965.

Jeff and I fought continually during the year we lived together with another couple in a four-bedroom Queen Anne house on Berkeley's Telegraph Avenue. Like me, Jeff had come from an alcoholic and argumentative family. Many of our conversations started with, "Why do you always, or why do you never?" I felt perpetually criticized for things I "always" or "never" did.

Though we broke off our romantic relationship after the first year, Jeff and I continued to be close friends. When he went to Africa, we corresponded several times a week. Like some couples, we were much better friends than lovers, and our friendship lasted for over 50 years.

***

In the fall of 1964, protests against the Vietnam War were increasing, and a keen sense of anger, frustration, and rebellion smoldered among our generation, many of draft age. Only our privileged status as students kept us out of the war.

At Berkeley, the introduction of psychedelics and the rise of hippie culture were catalysts for a major upheaval. It all started in front of Sproul Hall, the Greek revival administration building with a broad, terraced stairway leading to the entrance, just inside Sather Gate. There I registered for my classes and paid the then $700 administrative fee to attend a tuition-free state university.

It was a time of national turmoil following the assassination of John F. Kennedy and the escalation of a pointless and costly war in Vietnam. Young people were beginning to revolt against the stifling conformity of the 1950s, and psychedelic drugs were becoming widely available. I tried LSD one afternoon with someone who was sexually interested in me, but it wasn't reciprocal. In retrospect, it was the perfect set-up for a paranoid experience, which it was. After that I stuck mainly to alcohol, marijuana and an early, less potent variety of amphetamines prescribed for dieters.

The spark that started the campus revolution was a decision by the administration to prohibit all political activity and literature on campus property, including a table manned by the Congress of Racial Equality. This table and others could have probably been moved to the sidewalk outside of Sather Gate, but students viewed this ban on campus political advocacy as another unreasonable dictum from an inflexible authority. The revolt was on. Police were called, and a patrol car parked in front of Sproul Hall served as a speaking platform for Mario Savio, Jerry Rubin and Bettina Aptheker, some of the leaders of the rebellion. Savio had just returned from Mississippi, helping African Americans register to vote, and he was passionate about civil rights.

"There is a time when the operation of the machine becomes so odious, makes you sick at heart, that you can't take part! And you've got to put your bodies upon the gears and upon the wheels…upon the levers, upon all the apparatus and make it stop!" said Savio to an enthusiastic crowd.

The more the administration tried to crack down on the protest, the larger it grew, by now including the Academic Senate and much of the faculty. Among the students arrested for refusing to leave was one of our roommates at the house on Telegraph Avenue.

What I remember most was the free concerts on the Sproul Hall steps by Joan Baez, who seemed to embody the spirit of the time. Even today, her voice takes me back to those eventful college days, when a movement started that would spread to colleges and universities throughout the country, eventually resulting in President Johnson's decision not to run for a second term and changing U.S. politics forever.

Sometimes we went to class, and sometimes classes were cancelled, but eventually, the administration backed down, and things returned to a semblance of normalcy. I loved Berkeley because of its ferment, the quality of education and its beautifully landscaped campus. From the Campanile, you could look out over San Francisco Bay and see the Golden Gate Bridge in the distance. The smell of eucalyptus trees was everywhere, especially after rain.

I had read enough Dickens and nineteenth-century authors to have formed the idea that I wanted a "gentleman's education." Newman's *The Idea of a University* inspired me to get exposure to history, philosophy, science, literature, and the arts to understand our civilization and to learn to think critically. I also knew that a college education was my path for upward mobility. Fellow students from middle class or upper middle class families could be more cavalier about graduating from college, but I couldn't.

I set about exploring all of the riches available to upper division students, including courses in the Greek and Roman Classics, taught by German classicist Viktor Pöschel; Shakespeare and Renaissance English theater taught by renowned scholar Jonas Barish; Russian Literature, taught by acclaimed poet and literary historian Gleb Struve; Poetry Writing, taught by British poet Thom Gunn; the History of Western Music, taught by university harpsichordist and recording artist Alan Curtis; and Physics, taught by Nobel Prize winner Edmund Teller—just to name a few of my teachers. It may seem incredible to some that a Nobel Prize winner would teach basic physics, but that was part of the joy of Berkeley in the 1960s. To help support my living expenses, I worked in the Berkeley Library system, shelving books, updating journals, and labeling new acquisitions. Along with my academic course work, there were other lessons awaiting me at Cal and in San Francisco.

When I left Berkeley, enrolled in the English Honors Program, I signed up to write a paper on Gertrude Stein's *How to Write*. It was the literary equivalent of abstract painting. From a narrative perspective, it made no sense at all, merely repeating phrases and sentences with no particular order or pattern. No one else had attempted a critical review of the book. I in my hubris thought I could be the first. Since I was drinking every night after work at my first job in New York, I could never get around to making a serious effort at the thesis. Even cold sober,

I would have been challenged to say much that was meaningful about the book. The skimpy paper I ultimately handed in was rejected as inadequate, so I took an incomplete in the Honors course, simply graduating without *magna cum* anything.

Chapter 8
The Budget Socialite

*"High society is for those who have stopped working
and no longer have anything important to do."*
—Woodrow Wilson

I first met Philip Fay Stevenson at a party in the East Bay, across the bridge from San Francisco, in the autumn of 1964. Phil, who was a fifth-generation San Franciscan, seldom left the city. He had an apartment on Hyde Street with a view of the Bay, a landlord named Mrs. Bordas, and a charge account, usually in arrears, at the Searchlight Market down the street. One could hear the clanging bells of the passing cable cars at all hours until 10 o'clock at night.

He was a large and imposing figure. Because of his height, Phil carried his weight well—and with a little help from his tailor, often looked quite distinguished. His rather full baby-face belied his 40 years, except for a slightly receding hairline, which could be called a noble brow by a kind critic, and two small worry lines above the bridge of his nose.

His fingers had prodigious nicotine stains, and though he dressed with a flair, there was always a flaw—a missing button on his blazer, a frayed collar, a small rip in his trousers or a stain on his tie. At home, he was fond of costumes, especially of a silk Chinese lounge jacket with a high collar and ample sleeves. He often wore this when hosting a salon, sitting cross-legged on the floor like Jo Davidson's statue of Gertrude Stein.

Judging from the pile of books on his coffee table, the bursting bookshelves that lined every wall of his house, and his easy and intelligent conversation on a variety of topics, he read fast and copiously. He was opinioned on many things and an expert on food and San Francisco society.

I'm not sure if Phil graduated from college because he was always vague about his education. I don't think he had traveled much except for two years at Phillips Exeter in New Hampshire. Phil was a professional socialite on a shoestring budget. Phil's career as a socialite had a single goal: to marry someone with a sizable fortune. To that end, he had fruitlessly (and expensively) pursued a Nob Hill heiress named Abby Fisher.

Phil wasn't particularly handsome, but he was intelligent, witty, and charming. He had an encyclopedic knowledge of the San Francisco Social Register. He was a member of the Society of California Pioneers, an organization founded by families who came to California before 1850. He could tell you in detail who was related to whom and where their money came from. Phil could spin a good story and have an audience laughing in minutes.

He relished gossip, and his response was invariably, "Too funny!"

In the 1960s and 1970s, predating the rise of Silicon Valley and the enormous high-tech fortunes, San Francisco Society was an insular, provincial and cliquish group of a few dozen "first families," descendants of the Gold Rush and post-Gold Rush pioneers who had built the city from an obscure Pacific trading post to a booming metropolis and the financial center of the west. The old ditty goes, "The miners came in '49, the whores in '51. And when they got together, they produced the native son." Phil was the scion of one of the first families, unfortunately not one of the wealthier ones.

Phil and I immediately hit it off, and he must have decided to make me his protégé. For a blue-collar boy from suburban San Jose, San Francisco Society seemed to me to be the pinnacle of success and glamour. Phil became my mentor, and he soon had me dressing in Brooks Brothers blazers, attending the deb party circuit, the San Francisco Cotillion, joining the San Francisco Bachelors and learning about Trader Vic's, Beef Wellington and crystal match striker balls. All the while I led a parallel life as a Berkeley undergrad in the midst of a major social upheaval.

On many weekends, I traveled the 13 miles into the city to attend one of Phil's dinner parties, always a mix of socialites and social wannabes with copious amounts of liquor (top shelf labels refilled with bargain hootch) and a generous gourmet meal prepared expertly by Phil, who was quite a good cook. With Phil's encouragement, I pledged the DKE fraternity at Cal, which was the prestigious Greek house near campus. I liked several of the members, but I was never a good fit with the " bro" culture and casual indifference to school that were hallmarks of much of that world.

About this time, I met a beautiful young woman named Linda Forrest at a fraternity party. I was immediately attracted to her, and we began dating. Linda was more experienced than I was, and she introduced me to heterosexual intercourse at 20. I never disclosed that I was a virgin as far as opposite gender was concerned, but I found that I quite liked having sex with a woman. I kind of knew what to do, allowing for some differences in anatomy. Phil, of course, encouraged this relationship because he saw that appearances and marrying well were the key to a prosperous future. Linda and I had all of San Francisco and Berkeley to explore, and we spent a romantic year together, riding tandem bikes through Golden Gate Park and having candlelight dinners in the city.

Phil had a coterie of socialites and aspiring fellow travelers in his circle, some of them my friends, like Jim Rose, a fellow San Jose resident who played the theater organ and who worked days at Shreve & Company, San Francisco's premier jeweler in Union Square. Others included Ed Fiori, a prodigious collector of 78 recordings from the '20s and '30s who had an encyclopedic knowledge of the popular music of that era. Ed, who did not have a college education, went on to become a curator and archivist of 78 rpm records at Stanford University.

Another character was Harry Watson, a descendant of a San Francisco pioneer family and the grandson of William Sproule, the President of the Wells Fargo Express Company. Harry was a collector of private railroad cars and vintage autos, and he lived like Miss Havisham in three shrouded rooms of a rundown mansion on Nob Hill. It was a diverse group of oddballs, who enjoyed good food and drink—especially drink.

Harry learned that Phil was hosting brunch one Sunday, and he asked Phil if he could join us.

"I'm making an egg and bacon strata," said Phil. "You might bring some eggs."

Harry showed up at the door, dressed in a blue tailored suit and Hermes tie, two eggs cradled in his hand.

"A tightwad like his grandfather," said Phil privately to me.

It was clear to me even then that I lived in three distinct worlds: the activist, bohemian world of the Berkeley Campus, the fraternity/sorority circuit with Linda Forrest, and the society milieu of San Francisco. I suppose I was trying out several identities to discover who I wanted to be.

One day, the bill collectors and the landlord caught up with Phil, who had been living well beyond his means on a modest trust fund.

"I've been ducking Mrs. Bordas for three months," admitted Phil. Even though I sent her flowers I charged at the Searchlight Market last week, she's come this time with a marshal to change the locks."

He was evicted from his apartment, and I invited him home to our humble tract house in San Jose. My mother, always hospitable to a guest, made him dinner and gave him a place to stay until he could re-group and decide on his next step. He soon moved to a room in the rather seedy Beresford Hotel (we called it the Barefoot Hotel) on Sutter Street and a job next door at Hertz Rent-a-Car. I suspect it was the first paying job that Phil had ever had. Our small gesture of kindness earned me Phil's undying loyalty for many years, throughout my time in the Navy, when he was a regular correspondent, and many years later, when he traveled to New York to stand as the godfather to our first daughter Anne.

There are a few key mentors who have played an important role in my life, and among the first was Phil. Long after I had outgrown an interest in the Social Register and the superficial world of High Society, I continued to treasure his friendship and his many kindnesses. He was a prolific and entertaining letter writer, and I welcomed each missive from him long after I'd left the Bay Area.

Often, he would include newspaper clippings about some society wedding or scandal, or a letter he'd written to the editor of *The San Francisco Chronicle*, which provided some entertainment during my long hours at sea. Phil's critics, who dismissed him as laughable or bogus, often found they underestimated his resilience and tenacity. However ridiculous to some he seemed from a distance, he was always engaging and genuine up close—and loyal to his friends. Maybe that was the secret of his charm. He was a one-man finishing school for a young man from the provinces, rounding out an education that was to prepare me for my upcoming journey to New York.

Chapter 9

Taking a Bite of the Big Apple

"The most dangerous savages live in cities."
—Austin O'Malley

I began my romance with the city of New York while I was at Berkeley. Because I had transferred from Santa Clara, I had a few units to make up, plus I wanted to take additional courses in art, music and literature, so I spent two additional quarters at Cal, completing my degree in March 1967.

Between my junior and senior year, I received a scholarship to study James Joyce during a six-week seminar. We examined the theme in *Ulysses* of the son's search for his father, an archetypal motif that resonated with me personally—and, I think, with many young men in search of a masculine role model. But by the end of the seminar, with a little money left from the stipend, I decided to go to New York, where I was born and my father died—a place, I'd heard, where great and terrible things awaited ambitious young men.

I was neither a stranger nor foreigner to this city of my birth, and I felt I was coming home after a 16-year exile, to my father. His rheumatic fever as a young man damaged his heart. It kept him out of the war, but drastically shortened his life. I remember being awakened by coughing and a commotion in the kitchen one night in 1949, and my sister Elizabeth told me to go back to sleep. The next morning, he was gone, and I felt a profound sense of loss though I couldn't really understand or believe it was permanent.

For six days during that summer of 1964, we drove cross-country from Berkeley, two East Coast summer students and I, and arrived in Elizabeth, New Jersey on the steamy evening of August 29th. Elizabeth marked the end of the journey for my traveling companions, but New York was my destination, and so I caught the first bus the next morning into Manhattan.

***

A few weeks earlier, I had met Manhattanite Tony White in a bar in San Francisco. He was a public relations executive, and the City of New York was his client. He lived in a townhouse apartment on Sutton Place. Upon arrival in New York, I called his office in Rockefeller Center's Time-Life Building. He invited me to lunch at the trendy *La Fonda del Sol*, during which he gave me a set of keys to his townhouse. Finding the three-story limestone maisonette on an elm-shaded street near the East River, I opened the door and marveled at the elegant furniture and modern artwork, the rooms with soaring ceilings. Feeling welcome and at home, I soon found the liquor cabinet, poured myself a whiskey and awaited his homecoming.

I may have been only 21 years old, but I wasn't totally naïve, and I understood that sex would be expected in exchange for Tony's hospitality. I thought we might chat over drinks when he came home and talk about dinner plans. However, I was unprepared to be unceremoniously dumped into bed and raped without a shred of affection when he arrived. Sex was about conquest and dominance for him. It certainly didn't include any tenderness. In my experience, sex usually required foreplay and at least some kissing and a discussion of preferences. None of that was part of Tony's equation. He was only interested in penetration and orgasm (his, not his partner's). I was healthy and physically fit, but 3,000 miles away from home. In a city where I was still learning east from west, I was particularly vulnerable to abuse. I now understand the victimization of women when they experience a pernicious power differential, with limited options for resistance or defiance.

His carnal appetite sated, Tony headed for the shower. "I have dinner plans tonight," he breezily informed me. "You're on your own."

I realized the next day that I had to soon find an exit from this untenable situation, but while I was planning my escape, I drank heavily from his liquor cabinet and helped myself to loose change, saved in large glass bottles around his apartment. I dreaded Tony's return home from work, but I really had no place else in the city to go. Drinking was a coping mechanism for my anxiety and guilt about pilfering from his hoard of coins.

Two classmates from Berkeley had also traveled east separately, and I was able to rendezvous with them. My abusive host Tony also had a rental share in a house in Fire Island Pines, and he invited the three of us out for a weekend. Despite my misgivings, I had never been to Fire Island. My friends and I were eager to see it.

On our first night on the island, we discovered that we were each the main course for Tony and two of his friends. After much drinking, the game was on. I was angry, hurt and disgusted, not just because of Tony's brutal sexual appetites, but because he had talked me into inviting my friends to the debauchery.

What happened next was a total surprise.

Chapter 10

If You Can Make It There, You'll Make It Anywhere.

*"A father is a man who expects his son
to be as good a man as he is meant to be."*
–Frank A. Clark

After the experience of Tony White and his arrogant world of "chicken hawks," I was convinced I would never be happy in the chaos and cruelty of the city. But a few days before my departure, I met Stahley, or *Stay*-lee as he pronounced it. I first became aware of his baritone voice and mid-Atlantic New York accent from the opposite end of a 57th Street penthouse during a party, the details or host of which I no longer remember. H. Stahley Thompson was a barrel-chested man with gray hair and a receding hairline. He had a distinguished appearance, with a tailored blue blazer and a colorful Repp tie. There's a photo of him standing in front of one of the lions on the steps of the New York Public Library. He radiated that kind of authority. He was surrounded by an admiring coterie of men of all ages, drawn to him because of his natural charisma. He had a booming laugh and exuded personal warmth. His kindness reminded me that life, even in its harshest moments, holds promise.

I joined his conversational circle, explained my difficult situation to him and received an invitation to spend my few remaining days as his guest in a townhouse in the Turtle Bay neighborhood, a cluster of East River city blocks where Katherine Hepburn and a young Stephen Sondheim walked their dogs. Stahley had a two-story garden apartment, looking out at the Turtle Bay gardens, with a large bedroom and bathroom upstairs. Like Stephan Daedalus in *Ulysses*, I had found my Leopold Bloom.

It seemed inevitable that we would fall in love. He described me as his "godson" to anyone who asked, and he arranged a job for me in the American Heritage Publishing Company mailroom the following summer upon my return to New York. It was my entry level job to the history publisher that I later joined upon graduation from college as a copy writer in the promotion department. There, under the tutelage of master direct mail writer Frank Johnson, and working with the Art Department, I wrote book jackets, direct mail and other promotion pieces for *American Heritage* and *Horizon* Magazines and several of the books published by the company.

American Heritage was a powerhouse of publishing greats in those days that included the Civil War historian Bruce Catton, the biographer David McCullough, American Heritage Dictionary editor Oliver Jensen, and Native American historian Alvin Josephy. As a mail boy and a junior copy writer, I had the opportunity to meet and talk with most of them before I really understood how accomplished they were.

Summer weekends at Stahley's house on Fire Island were magical. Most Saturdays we were invited by neighbors to dinner, always followed by stimulating conversations with directors, writers, musicians, artists and rising stars in their professions. Still in college, I aspired to be like these rarefied creatures.

A House on the Ocean, A House on the Bay by Felice Picano is a favorite book about Fire Island because it supports my fantasy of Fire Island as a magical place, its darker side notwithstanding. Just 3.9 miles off the southern coast of Long Island and 2 1/2 hours by train and ferry from Manhattan, the Pines and Cherry Grove were the gathering place of the talented and the beautiful in the 1960s and '70s, when the Pines was still very mixed with locals and straight tourists as well as a small but growing gay population.

In those long-ago days, there was occasional animosity between the gay and lesbian communities. Not on Fire Island, where everyone mixed amicably as only exiles from oppression can. Each house typically had weekend guests, and houses, as a group, were invited to large, booze-filled and generally decadent parties, often with a theme, such as "Come as Your Favorite Celebrity."

Some of New York's top set and fashion designers contributed their talents to these events, and they were usually spectacular.

The daytime beach offered a continual parade of models, body builders, Broadway gypsies and other beautiful people to delight an observer on a beach towel with a good book and plenty of sunscreen. In the afternoon there were tea dances at the Boatel. At night, there were discos at a handful of clubs, and after hours cruising in a forested area between the two communities, known as the Meat Rack.

The magic of the island was its location between Long Island Sound and the Atlantic Ocean. There were no roads and no vehicle traffic (other than the occasional park ranger's jeep) allowed in these two communities on this half-mile wide sandbar. Everyone was linked by an elaborate network of boardwalks. Arrivals at the ferry dock from Sayville, Long Island, kept wagons locked up near the Boatel, which they could use to haul luggage and groceries to their summer homes. Water taxis were available between the Pines and the Grove.

Aside from the dock areas in the Pines and the Grove, there were no commercial facilities elsewhere on the island, so one could wander down to the beach at night under a canopy of stars, visible with so little ambient lighting, and listen to the susurration of the waves in peaceful isolation. As I looked out at the horizon, I tried to imagine what my future might hold.

I've been to Fire Island many times since those early days—with my ex-wife and my current spouse Gary. My long-time

AA friend Stan R. and I shared a room a few years ago at the Belvedere in Cherry Grove for an AA roundup.

But I have never quite re-captured the excitement, spiritual impact and beauty of those distant summers. Many of the talented and famous have moved on to the Hamptons or the Hudson River Valley, and I have grown older and less impressionable. But I was present for a moment in time in a magical place that will always be a beautiful memory.

My drinking began to accelerate in New York, living with Stahley. He didn't drink, but he had a fully stocked liquor cabinet, and I helped myself generously to his supply. I don't know if he didn't drink because of his Quaker heritage or because he suspected it might be a problem for him. He did call attention to my drinking, but I shrugged it off. To me, it was like medicine for my anxiety, as well as a social lubricant.

Stahley loved the *Sunday New York Times* crossword puzzle. He would start it on the way home from Fire Island on a summer afternoon and finish it by Tuesday or Wednesday. I would pitch in whenever he was stumped by a challenging clue.

My father figure and mentor, H. Stahley Thompson, New York, circa 1965.

There were a few mysteries about Stahley that have never been resolved. He would never tell anyone what the H. preceding his name stood for. At one time he confided to me that he'd been married to a woman, but he was never willing to discuss it again. He shared that he had been born on one of the last farms in the upper reaches of Manhattan, but I wasn't able to get more information than that. There was a guarded secret compartment in Stahley's life that was off-limits to nearly everyone, and his professional obituary several years later shed no more light on these questions. His kindness and generosity more than compensated for the mysteries.

Six months into our cohabitation in the city after college, Stahley gently suggested that I find my own apartment. He saw that I had a growing drinking problem long before I could acknowledge it.

"Joe," he said, "It's time for us both to move on. There's a 30-year age difference between us, and you need to spend more time with the young people who share your interests. I'm long past the club or disco stage, and I don't think you want to spend your nights here drinking and working on crossword puzzles. I've asked Human Resources to give you a raise so that you can find an apartment, maybe with a roommate."

Initially hurt, I came to realize the wisdom of this decision. Our intimate relationship, though not our friendship, was over. The relationship I had with Stahley was like the Greek practice of a mature man taking on a younger man as his *erastês*, mentor, and champion. We both shared a love for Greece. He had studied Classical Greek, something I was to emulate years later. He was the Odysseus to my Telemachus seeking my father.

I drove Stahley to the airport for one of his overseas trips for the last time and stopped on the return trip to Manhattan at the Sacred Heart Cemetery in Queens where my father was buried. Sun glinted off the once-polished inscription on his granite headstone, now worn by years of sun, rain, and snow. I focused on the inscription: "Joseph McCormack, 1901–1949, beloved husband and father." I felt gratitude for having known Stahley, almost as a silent prayer of thanks to my dad for the gift of a protector and mentor when I most needed one. It was an inflection point—a passage from my adolescence to the responsibility of adulthood.

Two weeks later, at a straight singles bar, I met a Williams graduate named Sandy Briggs who was looking for a roommate in an apartment on the upper east side. Sandy was to introduce me to the glorious fall in New England where he went to school.

Since we had a one-bedroom apartment on East 60th Street, whoever brought home a guest had first call on the bedroom. Sandy, with his eponymous tousled hair and bright blue eyes, was a babe magnet, so he often got first dibs.

This convenient arrangement lasted less than a year when I received my dreaded mandatory invitation from the Department of Defense.

Chapter 11
It's Not Just a Job. It's an Adventure.

*"Being in a ship is like being in jail,
with the chance of being drowned."*
—Samuel Johnson

The USS Newport News (CA-148), Flagship for the US Second Fleet out of Norfolk. I am in the bottom row, fifth from the right, 1971.

With 30 days to respond to my invitation from the Selective Service, I chose the Navy.

For the three months I spent in boot camp at Great Lakes north of Chicago, there was no liquor available, and I was able to dry out. However, if you coughed enough, you might get a small

51

bottle of alcohol-based cough medicine from the infirmary. It was a much-needed break that helped me refocus on achieving my goals.

With dry bunks for sleeping and hot daily meals, the Navy was a better bet than the Army, which could have had me sleeping in a Vietnamese jungle with MRE's (meals ready to eat) for nourishment. And the Vietnamese Navy wasn't much of a threat, with no aircraft carriers, submarines, or destroyers.

US Navy ships have been dry since Navy Secretary Josephus Daniels abolished the officers' wine mess in 1913. In theory, it meant we were unable to access alcohol when we were at sea. That also put a brake on my drinking for a time.

My Navy career lasted 3-1/2 years, but it seemed much longer, as time seems to do for young people. As soon as I graduated from boot camp, I applied for Officers' Candidate School. My initial application was rejected with the explanation that OCS was giving preference to candidates with engineering degrees.

My first tour of duty was on the USS Wilkinson, a destroyer in drydock in the Boston Naval Shipyard. Trained after boot camp as a navigator, there was no navigation to do, so they put me to work with a pneumatic tool, chipping lead paint off the hull. We had no ear plugs or masks, so it's a wonder I'm not deaf and brain damaged. The squad of class action lawyers apparently haven't yet been alerted to the Navy's lead paint issue.

Some of the friends I met in New York provided introductions for me in Boston and Newport. I arrived in Boston in September, offered the use of a corporate apartment by a decorator friend when I could get leave from the ship. This older, brown shingle building had a view of the Charles River and was surrounded by a canopy of trees at the breathtaking height of their autumn foliage.

"This is not so bad," I thought. *"I'm going to like this city."*

In Boston, I was introduced to the Brahmin gay social group who lived on Beacon Hill. Bill Phillips, a descendant of one of the city's first mayors, entertained lavishly at his tasteful antique-filled town house. Nat Perkins, whose family financed railroad construction in the mid-19th century and who were known for their philanthropy to Harvard and other Boston institutions, lived on Mount Vernon Street. His grandfather had won in a poker game (or so the legend went) an isolated, but beautiful camp on the Richardson Lakes in Maine, where a group of us sometimes spent summer weekends, hiking, and canoeing. We listened to the plaintive song of the loons after sunset under a starry sky with kerosene lamps for illumination and only moonlight visible around us. It was a sanctuary of silver and shadow, a world where time itself seemed to slow, and the only sound was the soft lapping of the lake, beating in rhythm with the pulse of the night. It was a welcome idyll from my daily duties in the Navy.

***

John Abbott, who was an executive with Mobil Oil, also invited me to his father's house in Little Compton, Rhode Island whenever I could get a weekend pass. Little Compton is a seaside community, a few miles from Newport, which looks like Edward Hopper's *Christina's World*. It's populated with New England brown shingle houses surrounded by stone fences and open fields leading down to the sea.

These weekends were drink-a-thons and often included John's fellow Harvard alumni and their wives from Pennsylvania's Main Line. I sometimes brought along a straight Navy friend named Mike Wilson. One night, Mike arranged a rendezvous with Marcia, the wife of a weekend guest who had long since passed out and gone to bed.

Mike helps Marcia over one of the ubiquitous stone fences surrounding the seaside property, deftly unsnapping her bra as he lowers her to the ground. Everything is quiet except for the sound of the surf as I sit on the darkened porch in the salt-scented air, nursing a nightcap. Marcia nervously keeps looking up at the house, which is silent except for the occasional snore from an upstairs bedroom window. John is on top of her now, making love like the sex-starved sailor he is, as she babbles, "Lud, lud, lud, lud…" Not exactly The Philadelphia Story, but a similar coupling of a socialite with an outsider.

My host John, like his friends, was a prodigious drinker, and he didn't hold his liquor well. One bibulous night, he fell off a stool and rolled headfirst into the fireplace. Two friends pulled him out by his feet and put his hair out with a seltzer bottle.

***

It was probably easier to get a Rhodes Scholarship than it was to get into Navy OCS, especially since so many Ivy League and top engineering school graduates were applying. I made a second application after starting a hometown newspaper service on my second ship, the USS Lloyd Thomas, getting the endorsement of Massachusetts Senator Edward Brooke and appealing to House Speaker John W. McCormack (no relation). This was also turned down with the same rationale.

I was certain that I was meant to be an officer, and I was determined to succeed, however many applications were required. About this time Speaker McCormack was implicated in an influence peddling scandal, along with one of his key staffers. Like so many political issues, it was a tempest in a teapot, but I wrote him a letter of support, which must have touched his heart because I soon received orders to OCS, to my surprise and to the surprise of many of my shipmates.

When I was admitted to OCS, we were again in a no drinking environment for 13 weeks. I had additional sober time, interspersed with weekend liberty, which was a license to drink to oblivion for many sailors and midshipmen. In short, I was no longer a daily drinker, but a periodic drunk because of my circumstances.

***

A chapter in my life came to a sad end while I was in OCS with the news from American Heritage Promotion VP Frank Johnson that my mentor Stahley Thompson was in the hospital:

"You probably know," he wrote, "that Stahley has been quite ill and in New York Hospital for the past six weeks or so. His white blood cell count has been excessively high, and the treatment to bring it down, which I gather is beginning to work, has been excessively onerous…I know he'd love to hear from you."

I was able to get emergency leave to visit him shortly before he died and tell him what an important teacher, father figure and role model he had been for me when I most needed one.

***

Because Navy Officer Candidate School was so selective, only the brightest and most accomplished applicants were admitted, and I felt inspired and motivated to be in such talented company. This has been a theme important to me throughout my life because I'm at my best when I'm challenged. Upon graduation, I was sent to the Defense Department Information School for Public Affairs (DINFOS) at Fort Benjamin Harrison in Indianapolis.

This was also a highly competitive program for all branches of the service, where we learned print and broadcast journalism, photography and other communications disciplines. At DINFOS, we partied as well as studied, and I began dating a Navy WAVE who was an eager sex partner. Julie was a dark-haired beauty who had been a novice in a Catholic religious order before she joined the Navy. She was apparently eager to make up for lost opportunities. All of us were in our 20s and most were single, so there was a lot of pairing up and bed-hopping in the Bachelor Officers Quarters. After a few exchanges of letters, I unfortunately lost track of her after school.

From DINFOS I was hand-picked by Vice Admiral Gerald E. Miller, then the Commander of the Second Fleet (and later of the Mediterranean Sixth Fleet), to join his staff in Norfolk. He chose me because I was a Berkeley graduate and a "Mustang,"—a man who'd come up through the enlisted ranks. Admiral Miller viewed the Soviet Navy as an existential threat to the U.S., and he tasked me with creating a briefing on the Soviet Navy and its fighting ships to deliver to enlisted audiences throughout the fleet. In preparation, I was assigned temporary duty at the Pentagon and given free rein to access classified files as needed. I did not take any files home with me.

The Pentagon is unique in its size and complexity—6.5 million square feet with five stories above ground, two levels below ground and five rings, creating a total of 17.5 miles of corridors. At any one time, there are thousands of civilians and members of every branch of the service, as well as foreign military personnel, on site. Half or more do not wear their uniforms to work daily so that Washington, D.C. does not resemble an armed camp. Navigating this behemoth was a major three-dimensional challenge, and every time I turned a corner, I seemed to run into a general or an admiral. If you're an ambitious career military officer, combat duty and duty in the Pentagon are essential for promotion to Admiral or General.

Upon returning to Norfolk, I boarded the USS Newport News CA-148, the last of the heavy gun cruisers, and the flagship for the Second Fleet. In addition to flying up and down the Eastern seaboard on C-138 military aircraft to deliver my presentation, I was assigned public relations duties aboard the ship, which included preparing a daily briefing for the Admiral on developing news stories and co-hosting a nightly newscast on the ship's closed circuit TV network with fellow Ensign Eric Eisenhower while we were at sea. I also attended public affairs officers' conferences and training sessions at Annapolis. In short, it was one of the most interesting jobs in the Navy to me and exactly suited my experience and interests.

I was eager to do more than public affairs, so I asked the Admiral for a division to lead as a junior officer.

Smiling at my request, "Granted," he said. "You are now the division officer for our journalists, photographers and the Second Fleet Band."

The Second Fleet Band was like a collection of misfit toys.

None of them wanted to be in the service, and all were musicians first and sailors second. Motivating them to do anything other than play their instruments was a major challenge. One day the Admiral returned from the local Naval Hospital, which had failed a cleanliness inspection, to ask for volunteers to clean the stairwells and back-office areas. I volunteered my division to clean over a weekend, promising them compensatory shore leave if they participated. Everyone stepped up to the task, which I led by scrubbing the steps like everyone else on my hands and knees.

The Navy's officer ranks during Vietnam comprised three distinct groups: Navy Academy graduates, OCS graduates, and ROTC commissioned officers. The best leaders were the Academy and OCS graduates, perhaps because their selection criteria were so stringent and because they worked hard to earn their commissions. The worst were the ROTC graduates. If you were an ROTC member in college in the late '60s, you were almost certainly out of step with the times, when protests against the Vietnam War were the norm on most campuses. There were some fine officers among this group as well, but many were fraternity boys and engineering students from southern colleges and universities, whose sense of entitlement and superiority did not endear them to the enlisted men. They just brought their campus "bro" culture into the Navy with them. They led with arrogance rather than empathy. The ubiquitous Filipino stewards were rumored to spit in their scrambled eggs before serving breakfast.

There is a saying in the Marines, "If you must use your rank to enforce an order, you have already failed as a leader." As a former enlisted man, I knew that leading by example was the most powerful form of leadership, and I worked to earn the respect and support of the men who served with me.

Among my best friends on the USS Newport News were Tom Popovich, a Harvard grad and a junior weapons officer, and Tad Herlihy, my roommate and the ship's legal officer. They both read widely and were interested in issues and ideas, not just scoring with women and getting drunk. I would rather have spent an hour of conversation with either of these two than an evening in the Breezy Point Officers' Club, where getting drunk was the norm.

On my trips to Washington, I soon discovered that there was a clandestine group of gay and lesbian servicemen and women who met for private parties in D.C. Many were career officers or enlisted personnel who mingled freely and without regard to rank. In those pre-Stonewall days, any deviation from the heterosexual norm could be a career-ender, so there were marriages between gay men and lesbians for appearances sake, and discretion was of utmost importance.

In 1971, the Vietnam War was beginning to wind down, and the Navy was looking to reduce its ranks. I had orders to a submarine squadron in Charleston, South Carolina, or the option to take an early release from active duty. As much as I enjoyed the Navy, I was always cognizant that my career could end abruptly if anyone discovered that I was gay or bisexual.

In a letter I wrote to my Norfolk boyfriend Tony Damron in 1971, I said, "Talking to a yeoman who worked for the Naval Investigative Service this afternoon, I discovered the Navy can have all your mail intercepted and read in Washington with a simple request form. Better sign your letters 'Sweet Jane' or 'Any Time Annie'."

Discovery had happened to a friend who was a Navy Captain and whose career was derailed during a background check to clear him for an assignment to the White House and a potential promotion to Rear Admiral. That was all the example I needed to prompt me to return to civilian life and to my previous job in New York. I remained in the Navy Reserves for a couple of years, drilling with a public affairs unit in Yonkers and putting in my annual two weeks of active duty, long enough to be promoted to Lieutenant Senior Grade.

The Navy had temporarily put some brakes on my drinking. Of course, there was always drinking on shore leave—and often to excess.

With school and my service behind me, I was ready again to conquer the Big Apple. I had had intimate relationships with men and women at that point, and I saw no reason to rule out half of the human race as potential romantic partners.

But first I wanted to explore my Irish roots and find the answer to a mystery.

Chapter 12

My Missing Irish Cousin

*"To be Irish is to know that in the end
the world will break your heart."*
—Daniel Patrick Moynihan

The bus pulls into Beggar's Cove, about 80 miles southwest of Dublin on a rare sunny Irish morning in May. Astride their bicycles are three young McCormacks: Bernadette, Patrick, and James, children of my first cousin Patrick, who lives with his wife Marianne on the dairy farm where my father was born. I'm a little startled to see that young Patrick looks a lot like me, with fair hair and freckles.

The story goes that all my father's brothers and sisters, except for my elderly, unmarried aunt Margaret, left for America in the 1930s and '40s. When my father's parents Johanna, née Maher, and Patrick (we have an abundance of Patricks in the family) McCormack passed on, it was either sell the property, which had been in the family for generations, or find an American cousin to run it, which is how the current Patrick became the heir to the property—as his eldest son would after him.

"Welcome to Kilkenny," says Bernadette, as we start our trek up a tractor-rutted dirt road to the house, accompanied by Shep, their dog. "Mammy and daddy are expecting you for dinner."

My first view of the property is of an eighth-century conical tower, possibly built during the Viking invasions for refuge during their periodical raids. It's this ancient feature that gives our farm the place name of "Steeple View."

The two-story stone house is tidy and trim, with cow and turkey pens, chicken coops, and a wheat storage barn with land stretching into the 200 acres behind it, punctuated here and there by stone fences.

The Irish are not big huggers, so a handshake suffices for our introduction. My bag is taken upstairs, where I have a bedroom with a view of the rolling green hills of the countryside.

Several of my Irish relatives in New York had mentioned my Aunt Margaret, who died unmarried and childless in her 80s. Looking around the room I saw photos and memorabilia of my deceased aunt. Opening a dresser drawer, I discovered a silver Christening cup, engraved with "Liam Michael," that must have lain there for 60 years or more. Although no one explicitly said so, I intuited from bibulous discussions with New York relatives that Aunt Margaret had become pregnant out of wedlock. In 1920s Ireland, during an era when the Catholic Church rigidly enforced its dogma about premarital sex, it was likely Margaret had been ostracized and shamed for her condition. It was a credit to her family that they nurtured and protected her from the condemnation of her friends and neighbors, but what had happened to her child?

I had always assumed the child had immediately been put up for adoption, which was the custom in those days. But the Christening cup led me to believe that Margaret had kept the baby for some time after its birth until its baptism. Then she had to surrender it to the church authorities. A tragedy from the past suddenly revealed.

***

My musings were interrupted by the call to dinner.

Dinner is actually the midday meal, and it's a hearty one with roast beef, a mountain of mashed potatoes and peas. It was simple, tasty, and filling. Alcohol is a part of every meal in Ireland, including breakfast, so I'm offered a shot of John Powers' Irish whiskey and a Guinness with my meal. I begin to understand why alcoholism is sometimes referred to as the "Irish disease," though many seem to drink responsibly.

Over the fireplace is a portrait of my grandfather Patrick, the first picture of him I've seen—dark hair, slight build and dressed in a three-piece suit with a riding crop.

"Grandad had some money," says my host Patrick, "but he lost it all on the greyhound races. However, the cows provide us with milk for the co-op and everything we need."

In the rarely used parlor are a threadbare carpet, a settee and a broken piano. There is a glass case with a stuffed pheasant and a stuffed badger, both of which had seen better days. Family life in Ireland takes place in the kitchen. The parlor might be used for the coffin of a deceased relative and the wake.

For supper, the evening meal, we have cold chicken with bread, fruit, and vegetables, much of it from the farm. Bernadette, 14, plays the accordion sweetly for us after our meal.

I don't have much small talk for my newly acquainted family members, so I ask lots of questions about the family and its history.

"In a couple of days, we'll be takin' ya to the family cemetery in nearby Tipperary, and we can tell ya more thin."

The next morning, I am eager to explore the medieval tower, now open at its base, although the main entrance would have been about 45-50 feet high, reachable only by ladder. Historians speculate that some 65 towers similar to the one on our farm, scattered throughout Ireland, were once the focal point for the churches or monasteries that grew up around them. They may also have served as watch towers, or, for the more spiritually inclined, as huge resonant systems for collecting and storing magnetic and electromagnetic energy. Inside the entrance is the sarcophagus of a knight in armor holding his sword with a dog at his feet. Could he possibly be an ancestor? The answer is lost to centuries of time that have passed. Nevertheless, I begin to feel a kinship for the first time to this land.

It's a Sunday, so we head off to St. Kieran's Church, the men and boys on the left, the women and girls on the right. There is no music, and the mass is in English, thanks to the Second Vatican Council. The sermon is about the brothers of the prodigal son and their sin of entitlement and righteousness. Since I identify with the prodigal son, I'm not too worried about the entitlement and righteousness part.

The pub is the requisite destination after Mass, where entire families gather for a meal and some entertainment. The owner, Mrs. Doherty, is the niece of its previous proprietor, who was a member of the IRA during the Troubles. I hear that one of my uncles was shot by the English Blacks and Tans, while crossing a field on his way home. I never learn if he was also part of the rebellion against the English from 1919–1921.

Our afternoon visit to the cemetery in nearby Tipperary County offers row upon row of headstones with my relatives, their surnames alternately spelled McCormack, McCormick or Cormac. Cormac is Gaelic for Charles, and the Mc indicates "son of." One brave McCormack served with the Royal Irish Regiment as part of India's garrison on the subcontinent where he met his end, probably due to malaria or cholera.

In Ireland, as in the rest of the British Isles, the eldest son inherits his father's estate. Younger brothers either work for their elder brother or they emigrate to seek their fortune elsewhere. Along with the potato famine and periodic social unrest under the British, it explains the mass migration of young men and women, including my father, from this country to America. I sense there's a library of history here of which I'm some small part, and it's somehow comforting to be returning to my father's home.

My home now, however, is in New York, where I was born, and I will soon be making a new and adventurous life there.

Chapter 13
The Return of the Native

"More than anything else New York is a city of superlatives, a place where the best, the brightest and the biggest is the norm."
–Marilyn J. Appleberg

I arrived in New York, after my visit to Ireland, with a "war bride" from Norfolk named Tony Damron, whom I'd met playing bridge during a weekend pass and befriended a couple of months before leaving my active duty in the Navy in 1971. We hit it off splendidly, and Tony soon decided to leave his high school teaching job to join me on our adventure in the Metropolis.

Someone once compared the energy of New York to the molecules in a hot solution, racing around at a rapid pace and colliding with one another. It was a stimulating and welcome contrast to the cynical drug culture of Berkeley and the bureaucratic pace of the Navy. Ambition and optimism were ubiquitous. The city lured with the siren song of self-invention, the promise etched on every billboard—"Be Anything. Do Everything."

We found a one-bedroom apartment on the parlor floor of a 1910 townhouse at 53 East 74th Street, a shady and inviting residential street. There was a Gristede's gourmet grocery store on the corner of Madison, where I once ran into Carol Channing, shopping for groceries, like anyone else.

Tony and I became solid friends and drinking companions. We had a comfortable physical relationship and set up housekeeping, buying our Ginori China from a discount outlet in New Jersey and an antique oak dinner table from a flea market in

Westchester. Our large living room with a fireplace became the perfect venue for booze-soaked parties with like-minded friends we made through the circle I'd begun to build before the Navy. Neither of us had gainful employment, but I had better prospects. By law, American Heritage, my employer before the Navy, was required to offer me a job upon my return from the service. However, instead of the Promotion Department, I was assigned to Sales, where I tabulated the results of our direct mail programs. The job title might've sounded interesting, but in reality it consisted of poring over lists and running an adding machine all day.

***

Because the Navy had trained me to be a Public Affairs Officer, I wanted to put those skills to good use, and looked for better prospects. I soon found one. After tracking down an employment ad and acing my interview, I was hired for an entry level public relations position with Rockefeller Center, Inc., the midtown Manhattan real estate complex of 21 buildings. My boss, the Vice President of Public Relations, was Caroline Hood, an early member of the Public Relations Society of America and a past president of Women in Public Relations and of Advertising Women of New York. She upheld the Center's culture of suit jacket and tie to maintain a professional image when leaving our individual offices. Miss Hood, as we called her despite her marriage to business executive John Carlin, had prescription glasses of every color to match her daily outfits. She used her glasses, like Meryl Streep, for a variety of dramatic gestures.

Our job in public relations was to keep Rockefeller Center in the press as a desirable commercial address for major corporations. The first and anchor tenant was RCA, which owned and operated NBC, which is still located at "30 Rock."

"Mr. McCormack," (we were all Mr. or Miss to our boss) she'd say, "Give me a thousand words on Morgan Stanley renewing their lease at 30 Rockefeller Plaza."

In addition to writing leasing stories for the real estate press, my fun job was managing special events for the Center, which included the annual televised Christmas Tree Lighting with celebrity hosts like Debbie Reynolds, a major fashion show on Fifth Avenue with Oscar de la Renta, and a Folk Festival with the newly established Museum of Folk Art, which required me to locate sheep for a shearing exhibition daily—no small challenge in Manhattan.

"Where are the wooly sheep going to come from?" I asked.

"Why, from wherever they are now," replied Miss Hood, "You might start with the zoo."

I coordinated many of these events, including the filming of a scene for *40 Carats* with Liv Ullmann and Edward Albert, Jr. which took place on the Center's famous skating pond. These events typically went past midnight and into the early hours of the morning to ensure that the film crew had unrestricted access to the facility.

Each year, we celebrated UN Day with support from the United Nations Association of the USA. Governor Nelson Rockefeller presided over the event, held in the Lower Plaza, where the skating pond operated during the winter months. Diplomats and representatives from the major real estate families of New York were always invited and given VIP treatment. The Rudins, the Dursts, the Tishmans, and Lawrence Wien, who pioneered the concept of real estate syndication with Harry Helmsley when they bought the Empire State Building. Notably, the Trumps, whose properties were primarily in Queens and Brooklyn, were never invited. Donald Trump was chiefly known then for getting his photo in the tabloids with his latest arm candy.

Other events included the celebration of ANZAC Day, a commemoration of the Australian and New Zealand casualties during the First World War (the Australian Consulate was in the Center's International Building) and the annual Yule-time Santa Lucia Festival with the Swedish Consulate, also a tenant. I can't remember the dozens of other events, from Thai Sword

Fighters to Sicilian Jug bands and Irish Folk Dancers, but it was a rich and busy program to keep the photographers and journalists engaged. John D. Rockefeller pioneered the new discipline of public relations with Ivy Lee in 1914, and the family were masters at its execution. I could not have had a better practical education in the field.

***

Early in my New York experience, I had met and become a part of "New Faces of (pick the year)". A group of gay Ivy League graduates, most in their thirties, were on the lookout for newcomers to the city with brains or beauty—or both. These weren't the chicken hawks of my undergraduate experience, but more of a social club.

Jake Lasker, the convenor, was a Harvard graduate from small-town Texas. He lived in a second-floor loft on Lexington Avenue across the street from Jägerhaus, a venerable German bar in Yorkville. The son of a dry cleaner owner, Jake was dazzled by his moneyed classmates at Harvard. Slightly built and balding, he had a ready wit to entertain his guests, and he gathered them regularly for alcohol-fueled parties in his loft. Jake was a copywriter at J. Walter Thompson—a highly desirable, if stressful—career in the Mad Men era. When we weren't drinking, we were playing bridge, a game I'd picked up during long hours at sea in the Navy.

Among our bridge-playing friends was a young attorney named Bill Thom, who founded Lambda Legal Defense and Education Fund in 1973 to advocate and litigate for gay equality. I was not a great bridge player, especially after a few drinks. My partners sometimes fled the table in humiliation. However, one night after a game of bridge with Tony and me, Bill announced, "The New York Supreme Court has finally granted Lambda its charter on appeal—after nearly a year." Bill and I created a press release, and using my Rockefeller Center Media Directory, we sent it out to dozens of New York outlets. It was picked up a day or two later by *The New York Times*. It was one of the paper's first references to the gay community that was not in a medical or criminal context. Lambda today is a powerful force for impact litigation that's advanced LGBTQ equality, and I'm proud to say I played a very small role in its beginning.

Drinking on the company expense account wasn't discouraged, and I did more than my share. Most of my young friends, including Bill, drank daily—and often to excess—on weekends on Fire Island or in the Hamptons. Tony kept up with me and, at some point, added drugs to his menu. It wasn't yet affecting my work, except for the occasional hangover, but it troubled me enough to offer prayers for help to a deity I didn't really believe in at St. Patrick's Cathedral, across the street from my office on Fifth Avenue. It turned out that prayer alone was not the answer.

Chapter 14

The Priceless Table

"The best things in life aren't things."

—Unknown

One day, Miss Hood, who bore a striking resemblance to Barbara Stanwyck, and who was the niece of center architect Raymond Hood, called me into her spacious, carefully decorated office, saying, "Mr. McCormack, this is Professor Anna Feldman from Columbia University. She is writing a book on the architecture of Rockefeller Center, and I want you to see that she has our full cooperation and any access to non-public areas she requires."

Anna Feldman was a small, slightly built woman with a high forehead and a friendly, informal manner. I may have been her local guide, but she became my teacher, sharing her extensive knowledge about the architects and artists commissioned by John D. Rockefeller, Jr. during the depression to build one of New York City's landmarks. I learned about the famous Diego Rivera mural in the lobby of 30 Rockefeller Plaza portraying Lenin leading the workers' revolution, which proved too controversial even for the open-minded son of one of America's leading industrialists. It was painted over and replaced by an anodyne allegorical tableau of American industry by Spanish artist José Maria Sert, who also painted a ceiling mural of a titan astride the lobby, which we referred as "Under the Crotch"—a favorite meeting place for our lunch appointments.

A key stop on our architectural excursion was a visit to Radio City Music Hall, a 6,000-seat theater that opened its doors in 1932. The Donald Deskey-designed lobby, with its soaring golden staircase and spectacular red and gold murals and carpeting, illuminated by ornate tubular chandeliers and sconces, is breathtaking upon first sight.

But the gem of the Music Hall—not open to the public—was an apartment on the second floor created for theater impresario Samuel "Roxy" Rothafel, who was instrumental in launching the venue for variety shows, and later, movies, in the 1930s.

Roxy's epic apartment, with 20-foot-high burled wood wall panels, floor to ceiling red and gold brocade drapes framing the windows, and walnut and aluminum tables and credenzas, was spectacular. Standing aluminum torchères flanked a 10-foot-high mirror over a mantel centerpiece, and a Steinway grand piano completed the living room.

"Donald Deskey was the Michelangelo of Art Deco Interior Design," said Professor Feldman. Since the 1940s the apartment had been used only by the Rockefellers and senior Center executives to host VIP events, and it periodically underwent restoration and maintenance.

In the entrance foyer was a small walnut table, supported by U-shaped legs balanced upon a pedestal. I noticed it, but I didn't give it a second thought at the time, confronted by the magnificence of the grand chamber in front of us. "It's uniquely beautiful, isn't it?" asked Dr. Feldman.

Over the next four weeks, Professor Feldman and I visited the many art works integral to the Center's architecture, from the Isamu Noguchi frieze over the Associated Press entrance to Lee Lawrie's Atlas statue at the Fifth Avenue entrance to the International Building.

One day, we were in the basement freight area of the Center, which linked all the buildings, an innovative idea when they were built. In a pile of used furniture—office desks, chairs and file cabinets abandoned by former tenants—stood the little foyer table I'd seen in Deskey's apartment. Thinking there must have been some mistake, I went to my boss.

"Miss Hood," I said, "there is a small Donald Deskey table in the abandoned furniture pile in the basement. It looks like it's destined for disposal."

"Oh, I wouldn't worry about it," she said breezily. "They periodically restore and renovate the interiors at the Music Hall and sometimes replace things as needed."

"Could I take it home?" I asked.

"Just fill out the paperwork for the maintenance people, and you're welcome to have it if you can figure out how to get it into a taxi."

I asked Professor Feldman what she thought the table might be worth. "It's a museum-quality piece by a famous designer with a clear provenance," she replied. "There's no way to put a value on that."

And that's how I became the owner of a piece of art deco furniture designed by an acknowledged master. It followed me from New York to Palos Verdes, from Palos Verdes to Los Angeles and, from there, on loan to my ex-wife in Virginia.

A few years later, a Washington, D.C. friend named Donald who had recently acquired a spouse, was setting up his own household, and he needed an end table. "I've seen the art deco table in your home. If you aren't using it, I have the perfect spot for it in our new house.

"I'm happy to lend it to you, but it's a designer piece from Radio City Music Hall," I replied to Donald. "Someday I will want it back."

"No problem," said Donald. "Just let us know."

More years passed, as I moved from place to place, settling eventually in a 1939 house in the Hollywood Hills. "That art deco table would be perfect in this new house," I said to my husband. "I'll call Donald and ask him to return it."

Donald was less than enthusiastic about complying with my request, but he eventually agreed to return it if I paid for the shipping from Washington, D.C.

"I know how much you love that table," said Donald. "So Ted and I had it completely sanded down to the wood and re-stained with a maple gel. There are a few dark blotches on it, but it looks like new."

"You did what?" I exclaimed.

I had kept in touch with Professor Feldman from time to time, purchasing the book she'd signed for me when it was published, and which featured a photo of the little foyer table from Roxy's apartment. I called her that night in New York.

Anna, you'll never believe what happened to that table from Roxy's apartment."

"Did you donate to a museum or list it with an auction house?" she asked.

"No. A friend, who had it on loan, sanded it down and refinished it."

There was a long pause.

I didn't know if she was going to be angry or upset.

Then she began to laugh, and I began to laugh until my sides hurt.

"Well, the table really is priceless now," she said. "In fact, it isn't worth anything."

Chapter 15

The Turning Point

*"Two roads diverged in a wood, and I—
I took the one less traveled by."*

–Robert Frost

I'll make a confession: I'm crazy about red hair and freckles. Maybe because they remind that I was also crazy about my cousin Andy. He was a year older than me, and we were the best of pals and more like brothers than cousins. When we lived in New York in the 1940s, my mother took a summer job at Greenwood Lake in New Jersey, and I spent the summer with my Aunt Anna and Uncle Bill in Pompton Lakes.

Andy and I were about four years old and we shared a bedroom in the attic, where a giant fan exhausted the hot summer air from the house. There was no air conditioning. Andy and I got into trouble together, exploring the fields and farms around the house, much to the justified concern of my aunt and uncle, as we'd once caught a nasty case of poison ivy while picking blueberries.

After high school, Andy joined the Navy. Unfortunately, he was "outed" by a shipmate who was somehow identified as gay by the Naval Investigative Service. In those pre-Don't Ask, Don't Tell days, any suspicion of homosexuality was immediate grounds for a less than honorable discharge from the service. Homosexuals were considered a security risk who could be blackmailed into working for our enemies, though there was no substantiated case that this ever happened.

After his naval experience, Andy came to California to stay with our Aunt Caroline, two blocks away from my mother's house. I reunited with him when I was home from college to find that in our attraction to other men, we shared a common bond.

We kept in touch over the next few years and met again when I returned to New York after my active duty in the Navy. Andy's experience with the Navy was one of my motivations for joining the Servicemembers Legal Defense Network board many years later to overturn Don't Ask, Don't Tell. DADT was, at best, a half-way measure before opening the armed forces to people of all sexual orientations and gender expressions, as many Western European countries had long-since done.

Andy and I soon discovered we had something else in common: an addiction to alcohol. On our last night drinking together, he invited me to visit his mother in New Jersey on Christmas Eve, which also happened to be her birthday. After dinner, Andy insisted on returning to the city, where some of his friends near his Lincoln Towers apartment were having a party. Against my better judgment, I joined him, and it was every bit as drug-fueled and inappropriate for Christmas as I'd feared. The raucous crowd in a small public housing apartment were blasting disco music, smoking joints, and sniffing poppers. The sole concession to Christmas was the tabletop artificial tree with colored lights and tinsel. I left very soon after arriving and went home to my apartment on East 74th Street. My boyfriend at the time, Tony Damron, had gone home to Virginia to spend the holidays with his family.

I continued drinking and woke up late in the morning on Christmas Day with no plans and no one to spend it with. I made calls to some friends, but all were unanswered or quickly dismissed with the excuse that they had other commitments. At that moment on December 25th, 1972, I felt as alone in the world as I have ever felt and seriously considered ending it all. I did speak to my mother in California, who was a help, and I set out to find a church service, but by one o'clock, all the services were done, and the churches shuttered for the rest of the holiday.

I decided to go ice skating at Rockefeller Center, where I was working at the time. Still a bit drunk from the night before, I was in no condition to ice skate, and I collided with another skater's elbow, getting a black eye for my clumsiness. After lunch at the rink-side restaurant, I managed to reach a Jewish friend, who was not celebrating Christmas, and he invited me over to spend the afternoon. An international ballet impresario, he lived in the historic Apthorp Apartments on Broadway and West 79th Street. In the foyer of his apartment was a larger-than-life reproduction of Michelangelo's statue of Moses. Like my host, it was very theatrical.

The next day, things returned to normal, but looking back on that Christmas many years later in sobriety, I remember it as one of life's low points for me. I felt alone in a city of eight million people. Sobriety was four years away and already I'd "hit bottom."

Chapter 16
Four Thousand Entrepreneurs

"Education is the kindling of a flame, not the filling of a vessel."
—Socrates

Rockefeller Center was a great place, if a bit old-fashioned and formal. The only path for promotion for me, however, was in the leasing department where they negotiated multi-year space for corporations that generated the income for the Center. It was a real estate broker's job and didn't hold much appeal. After a couple of years, I came upon the Young Presidents' Organization (YPO), and it was an entirely new direction for my career.

Barker Herr had been interviewing candidates for a staff position at YPO for a year before I was introduced by a recruiter. Apparently, my combination of experiences and personal background fit the bill. I was made an offer after a series of interviews with the Director of Leadership Activities and the Program Director. I had never heard of the low-profile organization, but I was about to embark on the most interesting and challenging job of my career.

Founded in 1951 by Ray Hickok, a Korean War veteran who inherited his father's business and who had scant experience running a company, YPO had grown to over 4,000 CEOs (who had become CEOs under the age of 40). In 1974, it had chapters in 45 foreign countries and a membership of high achievers and prominent leaders with significant influence. Today, it has 30,000 members in 142 countries.

Many U.S. members were Nixon-era Republicans, and some held cabinet-level and other important government posts, taking leave from their primary businesses. The mission of YPO was networking, peer-to-peer education, and idea exchange. There were three primary groups of YPO members: entrepreneurs who founded the businesses they led; sons and grandsons of company founders; and professional CEOs chosen for their skills to lead a major company. The last group was the smallest because it was unusual for someone under 40 to be chosen to lead a large, long-established company. But there were a few, like Don Fordyce at Manhattan Life Insurance, Steve Ross at Warner Communications and Sandy Weil at Shearson Hayden Stone. Other members included Howard H. "Beau" Callaway, Secretary of the Army, Federal Reserve Governor Jack Sheehan, and other prominent political appointees.

My job was to identify leadership opportunities outside of their business roles for members of YPO. This included a variety of consulting projects for the Federal Reserve, Department of Transportation, Department of the Navy, the Small Business Administration, etc. and to staff the project from inception to completion with the YPO members. It also included a project with the Management Institute of Iran, with YPOers teaching American business practices to Iranian business leaders. At the time, the Shah was in power, and there was a thriving business community in Tehran which welcomed us with open arms. It was my first solo assignment abroad, and it gave me the opportunity to tour Iran with stops in Isfahan, Shiraz, and Persepolis.

In Tehran, we stayed at the luxurious Hilton on a hill overlooking the city. In the lobby, I could listen to Persian music and order Beluga caviar from the Caspian Sea, offered from rolling carts with minced onions and toast points. I'm glad I had the opportunity to sample the very best on the company expense account, but I can't say it's a favorite dish.

Iran, like many Muslim countries, was dry—except for a few package stores typically set up to serve visitors. I made my way to one at the first opportunity to stock up on anything I might want to drink at, say, 2 am.

Our team leader came to my room to confer on our agenda, took one look at the array of bottles, neatly displayed on a shelf behind my headboard and said, "This looks like the room of an alcoholic." We laughed and laughed.

A week later, I am standing in the Persian desert among the ruins of Persepolis, which had been destroyed by Alexander the Great, thinking of Shelley's poem *Ozymandias*. Around me, the desert stretches in all directions. Our little group of visitors is dwarfed by the immensity and silenced by the stillness. I realize that I have never been so far from home. If I can find my way back from here, travel holds no fear for me. It was a moment of reflection and awe.

***

Back in New York, I identified board opportunities for YPO members with colleges and universities through the American Association of Colleges and Universities, as well as with community hospitals through the American Hospital Association. YPOers are eager to put their business experience to work for nonprofit organizations.

In addition to its leadership program, YPO held major "universities" each year, with one in the U.S. and one overseas. As a staff member, I participated in these all-hands drills in Bermuda, Hawaii, Hong Kong, and Vienna. These week-long events brought together world-famous political, business, and cultural leaders, whose expenses were paid to share their expertise and to network among the YPO membership and their spouses. The notable resources are too numerous to mention. They included such influential leaders as Alan Greenspan, Daniel Patrick Moynihan, and Charles Schwab, who was a member. I recall especially meeting Otto von Habsburg in Vienna, the putative heir to the Habsburg throne. At the time, he was the president of the International Pan-European Union, the predecessor to the EU. I thought my mother, who had been raised on a farm near Graz, would have been astonished at the company her son was keeping.

For nearly four years I worked with some of the most brilliant and talented colleagues of my career. Peter Tobia was a master strategist and tactician, and Ray Dee was a brilliant leader and wordsmith who taught me as much as anyone about communication, persuasion, and interpersonal skills. Barker, who had previously held my job, went on to other adventures.

One of my colleagues at YPO was David Gibb in the Communications Department. Curiously, I had met David when I was stationed in Boston with the Navy. He was a Yale graduate student, frequently in Boston and part of my larger social circle. It was surprising to turn the corner and find him working at YPO.

"David, what are you doing here? I asked.

"I was recruited from Hill & Knowlton," he replied. David would turn up again in my life more than once, and I'm amused that characters who have disappeared for a chapter or two, like in a Dickens or Thackeray novel, return later in an entirely different context.

When we completed a YPO university, the staff had time off and the opportunity to book some travel on the way back to New York. From Vienna, I visited Hungary, Poland, Romania, and Yugoslavia, including Dubrovnik. From Hong Kong, I made stops in Johannesburg, Pretoria, and Cape Town, with a visit to Rio de Janeiro on the way home. For someone who had always wanted to travel, this was a dream job for a young man in his 20s. Working with entrepreneurs convinced me that I wanted to have my own business one day, but first I had to find the right business. And I had to lose a job.

Chapter 17
Cooking for James Beard

"People who love to eat are always the best people."
–Julia Child

Raw. There was no other adjective to describe it. The crown roast of lamb, fragrant with garlic and rosemary, so elegant with its paper frills on each chop like little party hats, wasn't cooked. The guest of honor at our dinner party was famous chef, cookbook author and television personality James Beard.

Several weeks earlier we were at a conference in Bermuda, where Jim taught the cooking courses on American cuisine to the wives of over 400 young presidents, members of YPO, an educational association of corporate CEOs. As one of the staff members, I was responsible for wrangling the celebrity panelists and teachers and making sure they were comfortable and supported.

Coming down to the reception desk of the Hamilton Princess and Beach Club Hotel in the evening, I spotted a large and imposing man at six-foot-three and 350 pounds seated alone in the plush pink and green, chandeliered lobby, seemingly forgotten as the chattering couples gathered for cocktails and dinner.

"Mr. Beard," I said. "A group of us are going to try Blackbeard's Hideout, a seafood restaurant at the far east end of the island. Are you interested in joining us?

"Please call me Jim," he replied. "I would love to join you. I think I've had enough hotel food for a couple of days, and it sounds like an adventure."

An hour later, five of us packed into a rental car and headed east on one of Bermuda's two lane, serpentine roads, past villages of pastel-colored bungalows, far, far away from the conference. Blackbeard's is built on a cliffside in the shadow of Fort St. Catherine, an imposing stone relic of the British colonial period. On a window table overlooking Achilles Bay, we settled; the evening sky slowly turned orange, pink and deep purple as the stars began to appear.

Friends David, Barry and Jill were cheerful, if boisterous company, and we were laughing heartily as Jim regaled with stories of cooking disasters on his TV show, the first of its kind, a year or two before Julia Child began her televised program.

"There was the time," he said, "when I had a famous seafood chef as my guest, and I prepared a whole red snapper with wine and butter, wrapped in parchment paper. Unfortunately, the program assistant didn't know the difference between parchment paper for cooking and parchment paper for diplomas. The fish essentially fell apart after 30 minutes in the oven, and we were left with fish and parchment fragments soaked in wine. It was inedible."

After several similar stories, we were ready to call for our check. I mustered the courage to ask a bold question.

"Jim, would you like to come to dinner at our apartment in New York when we're all back home?"

"I'd like that," he replied. And the game was on.

At the time I lived in a five-room apartment in a pre-war building near Central Park with a real dining room. We set an elegant table with our newly acquired Ginori China, Stieff silver and linen napkins. Barry brought a beautiful centerpiece with orange mums framed with red and gold maple leaves.

Knowing that Jim Beard was famous for his promotion of American cuisine, I wanted the menu to be simple and elegant. He was also on a low salt diet, so I asked David, who had a comprehensive knowledge of spices, to make the vegetables for our meal. He decided upon broccoli rabe with olive oil and fresh peas.

Jill, who was a whiz at baking, would make a chocolate soufflé for dessert.

I would make the pièce de résistance—a crown roast of lamb from Pino's Prime Meat on Sullivan Street, one of the finest butchers in the city.

On a chilly autumn Saturday night, James Beard arrived on schedule at 7 pm. I put the lamb in the oven, setting the timer for an hour and 40 minutes. I asked David to start his vegetables at an hour and 30 minutes, and Jill to put her soufflé in the oven at an hour and 50 minutes.

After hors d'oeuvres and a few glasses of wine (maybe more than a few), I heard the alarm go off. Like the sous chef at a fancy restaurant, I began barking orders at my colleagues: "Time to start the vegetables," I directed. Pulling the crown roast out of the oven to cool, I instructed Jill, "Time to put in the soufflé."

After another 15 minutes, we were ready to begin. I brought the crown roast and the crisp, freshly sauteed vegetables to the table. Beaming with pride, I said to Jim, "Do you want to do the honors and carve the roast?" I handed him a sharp carving knife.

As he cut into the crown, I saw to my horror that the meat was brick red, blood oozing from the fresh cut. I had timed the five-pound roast at 20 minutes per pound prescribed for a leg of lamb, instead of the 40 minutes per pound, essential for a crown roast.

Jim must have seen the look of horror on my face. "I think it needs a little more time," he said.

Two hours later, we returned to the table. The roast was finally cooked, but the re-heated vegetables were the consistency of Gerber's green bean baby food. The soufflé, long since deflated, looked like the remains of an evening walk with my dog suffering from an upset stomach.

Deflated like the soufflé, I apologized profusely to the kindly Mr. Beard.

"At least you weren't serving your dish on TV, being watched by an audience of a hundred thousand," he smiled. "Thank you for inviting me to join you in Bermuda and for tonight."

* * *

On May 13, 1975, I realized that I could no longer do my challenging job at YPO and that I needed help. My two colleagues and I had been to Washington, D.C. for a day of meetings with government officials. They returned to their desks on time the next day. I wandered in about 10 o'clock because I had just continued my drinking when I got home. They could stop, and, once I started, I couldn't.

I was called on the carpet and told not to show up an hour late for work again.

I had been living alone in our apartment since Tony moved out, drinking each evening after work until I passed out—or went out at midnight in search of anonymous sex at the downtown deserted Hudson River piers or in a gay bar. In New York, bars are open until 4 am.

On a typical morning, I filled the sink with ice to wash my face in cold water, to wake up and reduce the puffy appearance of the "morning after." I'd take a couple of aspirin and board the number 4 train to work. I honestly couldn't tell you if it was sunny or overcast. If I hadn't arrived at work wet, it probably wasn't raining.

Most mornings I got little done except shuffling papers and pretending to be busy. At noon I would head for the Vanderbilt or Westside Y to sweat out the booze with a workout and a sauna. In the afternoons I was productive, but half of the day was over. At 6 or 7 o'clock when I returned home, I would start drinking all over again. In the beginning, it was a vodka martini or two with the evening news, followed by wine with dinner and brandy or cognac after. Later, it became a $14 gallon of cheap red wine, next to my reading chair as I periodically tried to read a few paragraphs in some book.

My world had shrunk to my apartment and my office. I refused most invitations because it became too much of a burden to socialize. My eating habits were unhealthy and irregular. I had put on some weight, and I was, in retrospect, clinically depressed. I felt exhausted nearly all the time. I had prayed from time to time for help *with* my drinking, but it never occurred to me to stop. I was seeking some way to control or moderate my alcoholic intake. Oh, I could stop for a day or two with some difficulty, but the first drink inevitably led to the second, the third, the fourth, etc. I didn't think alcohol was my problem. I thought it was a solution to my problems that had stopped working.

My primitive spiritual connection to a Higher Power, if one existed, was a barter relationship—I'll do this if you give me that. I had run out of things to bargain with, and I was defeated. So, that May Tuesday morning after closing my office door and realizing I was incapable of planning an elaborate overseas trip for YPO members, I opened the New York City phone book and found a therapist named Craig Evans on East 40th Street. For the first time in my life, I spoke to someone honestly about my drinking.

"Can you not drink until our session next week?" asked Craig.

It was a novel idea for me, but I agreed and continued to see him. Knowledgeable about alcoholism and addiction, Craig suggested I try Alcoholics Anonymous—too drastic a solution in my view. I had no idea I was about to begin my most important and longest journey.

Chapter 18
The Journey of 12 Steps Begins in a Basement

*"If you have faith the size of a mustard seed,
you could say to this mulberry tree,
'Be pulled up by the roots and be planted in the sea,'
and it would obey you."*

–Luke 17:6

In 1976, there was not a lot of public information about alcoholism. There were no billboards advertising plush treatment facilities or celebrities going public with their alcohol or drug problems. AA was a kind of secret society, and you had to be determined to seek it out, not unlike the gay subculture in San Francisco a decade earlier.

I was willing to concede that I had a problem with alcohol, but the term "alcoholic" described my long-deceased stepfather, who underwent a personality change and became hostile when he drank. That wasn't my experience. Even the fatal drunk driving accident in my college years seemed to me an anomaly rather than a part of a pattern. Finally, after resisting Craig's suggestions, I agreed to give AA a look and attended my first meeting at noon at Mustard Seed at 122 East 37th Street, a short walk from my office.

After rechecking the address, which was only six blocks from my office, I looked around nervously to make sure no one I knew was on East 37th Street. Such is the grandiosity of an alcoholic that I worried anyone would care, even if they knew I was attending my first AA meeting at an unmarked location.

Gathering my resolve, I entered an inconspicuous brownstone through a basement door. Well-dressed men and women milled around the room, along with other less well-dressed sorts, and even a few I presumed to be itinerant or 'down on their luck.' I didn't immediately feel at home.

My therapist Craig suggested I try a few different meetings among the hundreds each day in New York City, and I began to go to "Live and Let Live," the first gay meeting, at Yorkville Doctors' Hospital on the upper east side. There were also many mixed meetings in Greenwich Village and other mid-town locations, including the Christian Science Reading Room on East 48th and meetings at Fifth Avenue Presbyterian Church and St. Thomas's Church, where I was later to get married.

I stayed sober, felt better, and became a regular at AA. Then I flew to Hong Kong for one of YPO's annual international universities.

In Hong Kong, a co-worker said, "You must try the local beer. The Czechs built a brewery here, and the Pilsner is some of the best in the world."

I initially refused. The second day, I succumbed to temptation. It was only a matter of days before I was drinking myself into oblivion after working hours. With all the alcohol and food at my disposal as a business expense, it was an easy slide back into addiction.

When I returned to New York, an AA pal named Tim M. called me to check in from time to time.

"How's it going?" he would ask.

When I shared my plight with him, he suggested I try "controlled drinking" for a while to see how that would work out. I tried to "control" my habit by becoming a periodic drinker. Rather than drinking daily, as before, I tried to limit my drinking, sometimes unsuccessfully, to weekends. Sometimes weekends started at noon on Friday and ended on Monday or Tuesday.

You might as well suggest to a food addict eating one spoon of ice cream from a pint or one potato chip from a bag before throwing the rest away. I bought several self-help books that piled up on my nightstand to fix my problem, but I'm not sure I read more than a page or two from any of them.

One particularly low day, Tim called me and asked if I wanted to go to a meeting that evening. Not to hurt his feelings, I said yes. I still remember the date: August 13, 1976.

* * *

At the Mustard Seed meeting, I had struck up an acquaintance with Ralph B., a sportswriter for the *Daily News*. Ralph had on a tweed jacket and open collar shirt with a loosely tied tie and a pork pie hat.

Ralph said, "Your first time here?"

I mumbled something about giving AA a try at the suggestion of my therapist. Ralph was not particularly warm and not the least bit sentimental. Like many, he was a smoker. He hated the newly fashionable custom of holding hands for the closing prayer, so he lit two cigarettes, one in each hand, to discourage anyone's grubby paw from reaching for his.

He asked if I had a sponsor. When I replied that I didn't, he appointed himself for the job. He proved to be a steady and intelligent guide through the steps, and he became a trusted friend.

My sponsor Ralph was more a coach than a teacher, a guide through the 12 Steps, offering comfort in times of sorrow, encouraging me to overcome challenges, and celebrating my accomplishments and joys. He modeled a virtuous life and lived the promises of sobriety. He supported me to become the best version of myself. Ralph was all of that for me.

I spoke to Ralph nearly every day, sometimes just exchanging chit-chat, but when needed, talking through one of life's problems. In doing some research for this book, I looked up Ralph's obituary. He had been a Captain in the U.S. Army Air Corps during World War II and had been awarded two bronze stars for courage in battle and a purple heart, something he never boasted about or even mentioned to me.

An early friend in AA was Stan R., the son of a printing company owner and a society columnist mother in Lansing, Michigan. Stan had come to New York like so many gay young men to live an authentic life out of the closet. Before getting sober, Stan was one of the New Faces of 1964 and the Brains and Beauty crowd in Yorkville where we both partied. In gay AA circles, Stan was a handsome newcomer, desired by everyone. He was also a genuinely kind and thoughtful person, and it was my privilege to sponsor him while we both lived in New York. Now 80, he is still a handsome man and even more beautiful spiritually. We keep in touch from time to time and always meet when I have the occasion to visit New York. He is one of several lifelong friends I have made in the program.

***

Cousin Andy and I independently discovered the AA 12-Step program about the same time and attended several meetings in New York during that first year. But eventually, Andy decided that AA was not for him, and by the early 1980s, our paths diverged. He struggled with alcohol and drug addiction and lost a job in the IT department of a major company. Meanwhile, there were rumors of a new and terrible disease spreading in the gay community and Andy, adrift in his addiction, became infected. In 1979, French scientists and American biologist Robert Gallo isolated the "Human T-Lymphotropic Virus" (HTLV) before the disease it caused was named "Acquired Immune Deficiency Syndrome," or AIDS.

The last time I spoke to Andy was from my mother's house in San Jose over a holiday visit. We made plans to meet at his Bronx apartment upon my return to the city, but he cancelled the date for our meeting, whether out of shame for the shambles his life had become or because he was too ill or depressed, I never learned. Sadly, he died at only 55.

A wise person once said that alcoholism is giving up everything for one thing; sobriety is giving up one thing for everything.

Everything I know, believe, and practice I owe to AA. That may sound like an exaggeration to a lay person, but AA was the portal through which I accessed pragmatic faith, learned the importance of humility, and discovered a way of life that transcends the acquisition of property and prestige. It has taught me habits of healthy thinking that enable me to deal with anger, tragedy, and disappointment without succumbing to resentments or despair. Equally important, it has brought me genuine friendships, without strings, based upon mutual love and acceptance, which are such a source of joy.

AA pioneered the concept of one afflicted person supporting another with the same issue. We take this for granted today with the proliferation of so many 12-Step programs and other mutual support groups, but in 1934, it was a radical idea. It may be one of the great sociological breakthroughs of the 20th century.

AA is a kind of compendium of practical and spiritual wisdom for leading our daily lives with a measure of acceptance and serenity. An examination of the philosophical and spiritual antecedents of AA would include the New Testament, the *Nicomachean Ethics* of Aristotle, *The Discourses* of Epictetus, the *Tao Te Ching* of Lao Tzu and the *Pali Canon* of Buddhism, among many others. AA is not allied with Christianity, Buddhism, or any other sect, but it teaches that all spiritual traditions offer wisdom and that surrender of the ego is the path to peace. I once heard at a meeting that any plan will work except for mine.

In attachment is rooted our suffering. It also teaches that dwelling on the past, which can't be changed, or the future, which can't be known, are prescriptions for regret or anxiety. Only by living and acting in the present can we find some serenity. Two common sources of discontent for many are not getting the success we want—or getting the success we want and finding it empty of meaning or satisfaction. I've learned in AA it's a delusion that material success alone will bring happiness. Service to others is now my formula for peace and contentment.

How profoundly important the decision to commit to AA has been to my life! Only in retrospect can I see the terrible consequences in the lives of others from the road not taken. At first, the divergence is hardly noticeable, but a two-degree alteration of course by a ship at sea can make a thousand-mile difference at the end of the journey.

So it has been for me, and I have every reason to be grateful for the AA sponsors and colleagues who have helped and supported me along the way. A seed planted with my first AA meeting has grown into the flourishing tree that is my spiritual life today.

Now that I was sober, my life was to take an amazing new turn.

* * *

Rob and I met shortly after I got sober one night in Uncle Charlie's North, a popular New York gay bar. Not drinking, I found gay bars to be too loud, crowded and a waste of time until 10 minutes before last call when customers typically hooked up. But, now living by myself in a five-room apartment, I was lonely and in search of companionship as much as anything, so I dropped into Uncle Charlie's one night around 10 pm, usually the beginning of the night's festivities for most patrons.

I immediately spotted a handsome young man with dark hair, blue eyes and a preppy look. We made eye contact.

"Hi, come here often?" I asked with my most powerful pick-up line.

"It's my neighborhood bar," answered Rob.

"Do you want to get out of here?" I queried.

"Let's go," said Rob.

Rob and I began dating, and I found him good company, as well as good in bed. And so began a four-year relationship with this clean-cut undergraduate at Columbia, as I continued my early journey in sobriety.

Rob and I were a happy couple. Drinking was not important to him, and he easily fit into my new circle of New York friends, joining us for bridge nights and social dinners with other young professionals. We traveled together to California, where we took the coastal drive from Los Angeles, with a stop at Hearst Castle, the Madonna Inn, and up the coast through the Big Sur, Carmel and into San Francisco, where Rob, with his boyish good looks and prep school background, was a big hit with my socialite mentor Phil Stevenson and my college friends.

***

Back in New York, I was invited to become a part of Rob's family. Rob's parents were Helen and George. They lived in a repurposed mill, the historical center of Mill's Creek, a charming tree-shaded Hudson Valley village of 678 households, 90 miles north of the city. Surrounded by rolling hills and farms, boutiques line the one-stop-light main street, Hamilton Avenue.

George was a senior IBM executive, and Helen owned a Hamilton Avenue antique shop and a decorating business.

Rob graduated from Columbia and applied to Wharton, where his acceptance meant a move to Philadelphia. We parted a bit sadly, but amicably and continued as friends rather than lovers.

Chapter 19
If Opportunity Doesn't Knock, Build a Door

"The first step towards getting somewhere is to decide that you are not going to stay where you are."
—J. P. Morgan

Much of my work at the Young Presidents' Organization was coordinating management consulting projects domestically and overseas, staffed by Young Presidents who pooled their expertise to address public sector problems.

I knew that my time at YPO was limited because so many young people worked there, and the culture of the organization reflected this. The exceptions were our Executive Director and the Director of Programs, both in their late 30s. On the cusp of 30 myself, I was already feeling out of place. I learned about the business of executive search from one of our New York member presidents, and I decided to pursue a career in this field, akin to management consulting but without the MBA requirement.

I weighed the possibility of attending graduate business school after the Navy, but the expense and loss of earning potential for the two years required discouraged me. Also, after the Navy, I was eager to get on with my life in New York and not return to school. Recruiting for executive talent seemed like a good move in a post-war environment of new and expanding companies.

I met with several of the big established firms without any offers. I began interviewing with smaller firms, and I was finally offered a job at Collins & Company, a long-established search firm established by former Gimbels' senior executive Phil

Collins, who operated out of London. Collins's New York team was headed by Norbert Grant, and many of our clients were New York and New England banks, including Manufacturers Hanover, New England Merchants and Chemical Bank.

One bright and sunny morning I walk into the office—coffee and apple turnover in hand—and I spot a blonde, beautifully dressed fashion model sitting in the reception area. I have no idea what she's doing in our slightly shabby office, but we lock eyes for a minute, and I'm thinking, "Woof!" I can't say I hear violins playing, but maybe a bar or two of "Some Enchanted Evening" crosses my mind. We made eye contact, so I had some hope there was a mutual attraction.

To my delight, Patty was hired the next week and joined us as our research associate and recruiter in training. We would soon have a close working relationship and more.

Our motley crew included Bob Smith, a kind mentor who taught me about interviewing when he wasn't poring over spread sheets, trying to balance his creditors against each other to support the social climbing lifestyle of his wife and teenage children in Leesburg, Virginia.

Our boss Norbert was a wheeler-dealer who had a "special rate" negotiated with the Copley Plaza Hotel in Boston, where much of our business took us. Patty was a hotel guest the night of their big fire, a disaster that injured Sumner Redstone and several other guests. She later told me she spent a chilly hour on the ledge outside her sixth-floor room in nothing but a nightgown before she was rescued by the Boston Fire Department. My genuine concern for her safety and well-being strengthened our bond of affection.

At first our relationship was purely professional, with Patty doing the research to identify candidates whom I would then call about a job opportunity. I'd moved into a fifth-floor walk-up above a French gourmet food store on East 58th Street. Patty, more by coincidence than design, lived two blocks away. From time-to-time I would run into her after work at Smiler's, the local convenience store. Seeing her in jeans and a parka, rather than her Diane von Furstenberg dress and heels with full makeup, made her seem more approachable. Here's the thing: having been chubby and awkward at 13, I continued to have that unconscious self-image, and I didn't have the confidence I was that attractive. Somehow, that mattered less for one-night stands or short-term relationships. Without the Dutch courage of alcohol, I had limited confidence for wooing a beautiful woman.

Patty and I spent many hours working together, so it was inevitable that we got to know one another. We became friends and discussed our personal lives, including the fact that both of us had had relationships with men and women. That became a unique bond between us because I had never been candid about that with a female partner. I had also never met a woman who considered herself bisexual.

This shared experience was important to what happened next.

Chapter 20
Recruiting the Perfect Candidate

"Sometimes the least expected love comes at the right moment, at the time you are ready."

—*Unknown*

I had been at Collins & Company for two years when I heard that the public accounting firm Ernst & Young had kicked off a new executive recruitment branch.

I was hired as a manager, which is two steps below partner, and we were off and running. The firm fed me a steady flow of search business, so I didn't have to hustle to bring in new clients, but I learned the fundamentals of search as a consulting practice to augment my on-the-job training at Collins & Company. The Big Eight, as the public accounting firms were then known, were strong believers in training and continuing education.

In those pre-internet days, research was largely a library activity, along with some rudimentary exploration of databases. Arthur Young (as it was then known) had a whole floor of workers with library science degrees and IT backgrounds to generate research information. Any laptop owner can now get as much in an hour on the internet. As the firm was building its research capacity, I recommended Patty from Collins & Company as a candidate.

I finally got up the courage to ask Patty out on our first date. I had tickets to *Romeo and Juliet* at the New York City Ballet, and we had front row seats on the balcony.

A couple of weeks later, I invited her home after a date, and we spent the night together on my pull-out sofa in front of the cozy fireplace listening to Harry Nilsson singing American song book classics on his 1972 album, "A Little Touch of Schmilsson in the Night." It was as romantic an album as has ever been recorded by a singer with a dulcet voice.

Falling in love was never in my plan. Until one day I realized I had.

Bisexuality is often dismissed as confusion or a stage one goes through before fully coming out of the closet. That was never true for me or countless others. As Loretta Young said, "Love isn't something you find. Love is something that finds you."

Our first year living together was the stuff of bodice buster novels. We drove to Williamstown, Massachusetts, where my old roommate Sandy Briggs had gone to college, to share the stunning, multicolored beauty of a New England autumn. We booked a seaside room on Fire Island in the summer, enjoying its beautiful beach and watching the sunset from the Fire Island Pines dock that seemed plucked from a romantic movie set on a tropical island. We took full advantage of New York City's abundant (and many free) cultural riches, including the Sunday Bach cantatas at Holy Trinity Lutheran Church on Central Park West, Shakespeare in the Park, as well as a dozen great shows on Broadway. Patty came to hear me speak for my fifth AA anniversary at the Sunday High Noon meeting in Sheridan Square. A well-known actor from *How to Succeed in Business Without Really Trying* was in the front row.

Patty introduced me to her godmother and her husband, who lived on the upper east side and who were also in the AA program. They apparently gave me the thumbs-up. It seemed I had met my soul mate.

After several relationships with men and women—mostly short-term—this relationship with a woman was the deepest and most meaningful of my life. Now in my mid-thirties and early business career, it somehow completed me, much as my relationship with my father-figure Stahley Thompson had filled an important need for me on the cusp of adulthood.

After five years of sobriety, I was now completely free to act on my attraction to women and to make a commitment. I swear I had the biological clock attributed to many women that it was time to find a mate and reproduce.

I had dated several eligible women who were feeling the same imperative, without making a meaningful connection until I met Patty. She was in every respect the perfect one—beautiful, intelligent, strong, and above all, highly competent and independent. I loved and respected her for that strength.

My friends were genuinely happy for me and supportive. I was to ask one to be part of our wedding.

Chapter 21
Captured by French Vogue

"Count as Blessing Every Day That Fate Allows You"
—Horace 65–8 B.C.E.

I sang with New York's University Glee Club twice a year in white tie and tails.

Our performances were enhanced by a couple of ringers from the Yale Whiffenpoofs or the Penn Glee Club who sang the solos, and we frequently went out to dinner in full dress after a concert.

After our performance at Carnegie Hall one crisp September evening, Patty, Rob with his date, and I traveled by taxi downtown to the Empire Diner, a trendy converted rail car with aluminum siding and florescent lights, where we were—to say the least—overdressed.

By coincidence, French Vogue was doing a fashion shoot at the location with models in evening dress, and they were delighted to discover us as unpaid scenery for their photography. Several weeks later, we anxiously awaited the magazine to appear on the newsstands. Sure enough, there were Patty, Rob and I featured in formal attire behind the sultry models, probably strung out on coke. We never learned their names. Rob, however, will forever be immortalized, dressed in black tie, in French Vogue.

There were more good times for the three of us. Rob's mother Helen volunteered to brighten up the fifth-floor art deco apartment Patty and I now shared on East 56th Street. Rob's parents and his younger brother Chris were all invited to our wedding.

We were both busy with our work. As sometimes happens, our social lives diverged, as I became more involved with Patty's family and circle of friends. When I received Rob's unexpected dinner invitation a year later, I was glad to reconnect with my old pal again. Now a bank executive with his Wharton degree, Rob never looked more handsome. He had matured into a young professional, and he had all the potential for great success.

Chapter 22
And Baby Makes Three

"Children make you want to start life over."
—*Muhammed Ali*

A year into our relationship, I gave up my fifth-floor walk-up and moved in with Patty at 141 East 56th Street, a seven-story apartment building with an art deco façade. With Patty and I both working at Arthur Young, we weren't sure how our relationship would be perceived by the partnership, so we took alternate routes to work, which was a walkable 10 blocks away on Park Avenue.

Patty invited me home to meet her parents Anne and George at their Hill Country retreat on the Guadalupe River. On my first visit to Texas, I had a glimpse of life in the slow lane in the rolling hills about 20 miles west of Kerrville. The house was built on a bank above the river, and the floor to ceiling windows overlooked the flowing stream and an occasional passerby on an inner tube, a popular pastime for the locals. For excitement, there was Crider's, an authentic cowboy bar that offered an evening of line dancing and the Texas two-step. On weekends, the dance floor was populated by guys in jeans with big belt buckles and Stetsons, holding a gal with one hand and a long-necked beer with the other.

I read in novels that a man was supposed to ask the permission of a girl's father to marry, so I rehearsed my speech: "I plan to ask Patty to be my wife, and I want to do so with your knowledge and consent. We both want very much to have your blessing before we set a date."

Said her father George, "Anne and I are just delighted about you and Patty. The picture of you two is on the living room desk, and we proudly show it to all who visit. Patty is very special to us, and we are happy to welcome you into the family."

And they were true to their word.

Living together in New York proved to be an easy arrangement, and on Valentine's Day, I booked us dinner at the Top of the Sixes, a top floor restaurant at 666 Fifth Avenue, with a view of Saint Patrick's Cathedral across the street, the very same cathedral where I first asked an unknown Higher Power for help with my drinking.

We had tickets to a Broadway show that had unexpectedly closed, so we spontaneously bought two tickets to *The Mousetrap*, starring Christopher Reeve, aka Superman. After the theater, and somewhere between the main course and dessert, I got down on one knee and offered Patty the engagement ring (with a very modest diamond) from Tiffany with my proposal.

To my delight, she said "yes." The other diners applauded softly.

It soon became known at Arthur Young that we were a couple, and there was support all around. The next few months were all about planning our wedding, which was to take place in St. Thomas's Episcopal Church on Fifth Avenue. As Patty and I planned our wedding, I thought of my old friend Rob and asked if he would be my best man. He agreed. It was all terribly civilized, without any secrets, and amiability all around.

Never having been married before, I suggested, maybe a bit inconveniently, that we make it a black-tie evening event. I decided to dress up for the occasion. It was in every respect a wonderful wedding, with my mother and other family members in New York for the occasion. The service was performed with his plummy British accent by Father John Andrew, then the rector of St. Thomas's and (as he frequently told you), the former confessor to the Prince of Wales, now King Charles III. We had a string quartet from Juilliard, and my last boyfriend Rob was the best man.

I treasured my closeness with Patty's talented family. I felt I had been initiated into a rarified society of high achievers. The parent generation were doctors, lawyers, investors, and bankers. Our generation—the cousins—were on their own path to achieving success. They were old Houston money and prominent citizens of Boston, New York, and Chicago. I was accepted and welcomed without reservation. I felt honored to be part of this clan. They were without exception warm, funny, and friendly. I hadn't just married an intelligent and beautiful woman; I had married into an exceptional network of people. Ironically, we had our reception at New York's Union League Club, and the Texans danced to the Manhattan Rhythm Kings and celebrated under the portrait of Abraham Lincoln.

Several months after our marriage, Patty became pregnant with our first daughter Anne. I accompanied Patty to New York Hospital on East 68th Street and York Avenue where she endured something like 14 hours of labor. Shortly after 10 pm, Annette McCormack was born. After making sure Patty was well taken care of, I walked the 15 blocks home to our apartment, stopping for a quick dinner at a Thai restaurant along the way. It was my first experience with Thai food, which was still something of a novelty in those long-ago days. But it seemed a fitting meal for a new phase of my life.

I can't describe the sense of elation I felt at having helped bring a new human being into the world. I was present in the delivery room and cut the umbilical cord. It all seemed very miraculous to me—because it was.

More miracles, as well as tragedies, were in store.

My wife Patty and me with baby Anne in New York, 1982.

Chapter 23
My Best Man

*"At his best, man is the noblest of all animals;
separated from law and justice he is the worst."*
—*Aristotle*

"I have HIV," announced Rob over dinner. The confession came at the River Café, a dining spot under the Brooklyn Bridge with a postcard view of the Manhattan skyline across the water.

"How? Who?" I asked.

"I'd rather not go into that," said Rob. "The question is what do I do now?"

I struggled to find any advice or suggestions. Rob was one of the most careful and least promiscuous young men I knew, so this came as a shock.

"There's new research on antivirals everywhere. We need to find you the best doctors." I hoped he would not run out of time before medical research discovered an effective treatment for AIDS.

***

It wasn't long after our dinner in the River Café that Rob contracted pneumonia, and his health began to deteriorate rapidly. He quit his bank job and took a low-stress sales job at Brooks Brothers on Madison Avenue. I was a bit chagrined to see him so underemployed, but I understood the reasons for his decision.

A few months later, Rob's new boyfriend Allen invited Patty and me, now married, for dinner at their condo in Chelsea. When we arrived, Rob answered the door. I was shocked to see an emaciated and tired looking version of the friend who had seemed so healthy and robust six months before. His clothes hung on him. I did what we did in those days and said nothing, giving no indication that I recognized anything wrong, all the time grieving for him silently.

Soon after, Rob died quietly in his sleep. Rob's mother Helen, with whom we kept in touch, sent us the invitation to the Frank E. Campbell funeral home in Chelsea, where 25 or 30 of Rob's friends and family members gathered to say goodbye. There was an open casket, and the mortician had done a reasonable job of making Rob look healthy. But I was surprised to see that this 30-year-old man's hair had turned nearly completely gray. Such were the ravages of the AIDS virus during the worst years of the pandemic.

After the service, I said to Helen, "Rob sold me the shoes I'm wearing."

She smiled sadly. "Rob could sell anything to anyone," she replied. I gave her a hug, and it was the last time we saw each other.

***

Several years later I heard from a mutual friend that Rob's father had died suddenly of a heart attack, whether this was brought on by his son's tragic end, I never knew. Rob's younger brother Chris, now his widowed mother's sole remaining child, went to the World Trade Center for a job interview on the morning of 9/11 and perished. It was another seemingly random lightning strike, unexpected and undeserved.

I thought of reaching out to Helen, but so much time had passed, and I was at a loss for words of comfort to offer her. How tragic the end for a happy family with two intelligent and handsome boys, both lost so long before their time!

From time to time, I open that old copy of French Vogue, and I see Rob again, smiling as he was that happy night. I grieve for the lives of so many AIDS patients, their future lost to this terrible disease. AIDS was to be the impetus for my future work and calling, but that was still several years and a continent away.

Chapter 24
The City of Sunshine & Flowers

*"Build your own dreams,
or someone else will hire you to build theirs."*
–Farrah Gray

As a new father, I felt a joy I'd never known before. I continued to make AA meetings and friends an important part of my life.

Patty and I walked Anne in her stroller to a park along the East River near 59th Street. Returning home one day, Anne was covered with the soot of New York. It was then we began to plan a move. By this time, I had a new position as Vice President with Billington, Fox & Ellis, a search firm founded by three Booz Allen alumni in Chicago in 1972. They lured me away from Arthur Young with a raise and an all-expense paid company car, an unbelievable luxury in Manhattan.

Billington had offices in Chicago, New York, San Francisco, and Los Angeles. I requested a transfer to the Los Angeles office, managed by Peter McLean. Peter advised us to look for housing in the South Bay, a good place to raise a family, albeit an hour's drive from the office, then in the mid-century Ahmanson Building in the mid-Wilshire Boulevard district.

We initially rented a two-bedroom condominium on Stonewood Court on Western Avenue in San Pedro, the port and fishing village of Los Angeles. By New York standards, we had enormous space at a bargain price. We had a view of the rolling hills of a cemetery from our bedroom window, and, of course, it was very quiet at night. I used to joke that it was initially hard to sleep without the sound of traffic, the noise of garbage trucks grinding up wine bottles and the occasional siren or homeless person screaming at night. I imagined recreating these soothing sounds as cassettes for ex-pat New Yorkers.

One day on a walk around our condo complex, Patty met Marty Powell, a neighbor with a baby boy about Anne's age. They soon became good friends, and I became friends with her husband Alex, an attorney. After about a year, our Realtor Mitzi Ray found us an affordable four-bedroom house on Palos Verdes Drive North. The Palos Verdes peninsula was one of the most desirable residential areas of Los Angeles. Marty, Alex, and Andy soon followed with a house of their own. We paid $210,000 for our "starter" home, which I thought was an absurdly high price at the time.

We began to make friends and settle into our new community. Meanwhile, we were facing the 1982 high tech recession, and Billington decided to close its Los Angeles office, as did several other search firms. They offered to take us back to New York or to join the team in San Francisco, but we were becoming happily settled in Los Angeles and wanted to stay in Southern California. With our new family to support, I went in search of another job, and the only search firm in Los Angeles that was hiring was Fred Hayden & Associates in West Los Angeles. Hayden & Associates was an Arizona-based national search firm with a Los Angeles office managed by Tom Spears.

West Los Angeles was a terrible commute from Palos Verdes, up the 405 corridor and past all the aerospace companies, which employed over 100,000 people, in El Segundo and the Los Angeles Airport area. I tried leaving home at 6 am or earlier to beat some of the traffic, but there was no good time to drive north on the 405 Freeway in the morning—or, for that matter, in the evening heading south and home. I found that my commute added at least three hours to my workday.

It was not a happy match for me. The L.A. office had six consultants, including me, and the managing director, who was quite possibly the worst leader I had ever encountered in my business experience. I had been a rising star at Billington, Fox & Ellis, but my business contacts were primarily in New York, so it took me a while to cultivate client contacts in Southern California. This was a challenge whose dimension entirely escaped the boss. His response was to micro-manage my time, monitor my phone calls, insist that I keep my office door open and call me on the carpet daily for some "constructive criticism." The other consultants were in the habit of offering daily praise to our boss, a form of sycophancy that I found loathsome. I grew to really dislike the man.

The boss's wife had a financial consulting practice, and we were invited to an obligatory combined Christmas party my first year with the firm, where I suspected there was not only a lot of drinking, but cocaine use as well. Patty and I found the whole crowd thoroughly repulsive. The combination of my daily commute and the hostile work environment combined to create a crisis of self-confidence for me. But I had surrendered my right to chemical peace of mind. One day, after my usual dressing down, I closed my office door and just sobbed, realizing I could never please the bully who "managed" the office.

One of my clients was MAI/Basic Four, a manufacturer of mid-size computers, at a time when files were centralized in many offices, with only monitors on individual desks. The director of human resources was Jerry Farrow, for whom I had done several searches. Jerry was a Naval Academy graduate, a Marine helicopter pilot in Vietnam and an enthusiastic sailor. We discussed the possibility of starting our own search practice, and one Saturday we met on his sailboat in Dana Point and sketched out a business plan. I was 39 at this point and mindful that the young presidents I had worked for had all become entrepreneurs or successor CEOs before the age of 40. Jerry and I each contributed $10,000 to our venture, and soon we were in business in an executive suite on Ocean Boulevard in Long Beach, about a 20-minute commute from my home.

A friend at Spencer Stuart referred our first piece of business to us—a search for an executive assistant for the managing partner of a law firm. It wasn't exactly a dream assignment, but it started to bring in the revenue we needed to pay our monthly rent.

Within a few years, we had a successful practice that included financial services, healthcare, and high technology clients. After moving the office to Costa Mesa, we added three additional search consultants to our practice. I opened a satellite office in Torrance and commuted to Orange County a couple of days a week. Among our regular clients was First Interstate Bank in Los Angeles, Group Health Cooperative of Puget Sound in Seattle, Little Company of Mary Hospital in Torrance and multiple high tech and aerospace companies. We were doing well, and there was hardly a cloud on the horizon.

Chapter 25
The Children Serve Us Spaghetti

*"Children remind us to treasure the smallest of gifts,
even in the most difficult of times."*

–Allen Klein

Patty and I had two girls: Annette, who was born in New York Hospital, and Caroline, who was born in California. By the time we left New York for Los Angeles, Anne was already six months old.

Patty with Caroline and Anne.

Caroline came along when we still lived on Palos Verdes Drive North, a roomy, comfortable, if somewhat dowdy house that was our starter home on the peninsula's main thoroughfare.

Patty's mother came west to help with the baby and Anne, who was now a two-year-old toddler.

Our Palos Verdes Drive North house was the first of three, each bigger than the last. We moved up to Via Pima and finally to Via Navajo, an architect-designed traditional masterpiece with Chinese silk wallpaper and a view of the Los Angeles basin. The previous owner of Via Navajo had gone through a bitter divorce. Despite the beauty of the house, I sometimes wonder if there isn't a negative vibe in a house that has seen so much anger and pain.

I enjoyed being a husband and dad. Patty joined the Palos Verdes Juniors (our local version of the Junior League), and she became active with St. Francis Episcopal Church, which was our local parish. I volunteered for an organization to renovate the Palos Verdes Beach and Athletic Club, a seaside pool built in 1930, which had been abandoned and was in disrepair. We made friends with other young couples, some of whom were doctors and lawyers, the typical professionals you'd expect to meet in an upscale residential community.

But there was also a fireman/electrician named Ian and his wife, Mary, who became friends. We connected over the Indian Princesses, a recreational organization for dads and daughters. We spent a three-day weekend camping on the island of Catalina, about 40 miles off the coast of California. One of the men in our bunk bed-filled cabin snored like a ripsaw tearing into a redwood log.

"Do you think we could smother him with a pillow and claim he had a heart attack during the night?" asked Ian.

"You're a paramedic as well as a fireman," I replied. "You would have to fake a heroic attempt to revive him—with mouth-to-mouth resuscitation."

"Yuck," said Ian.

We both decided doing nothing was best and resigned ourselves to some sleepless nights. Before lights out, we sat around a campfire with our snoring bunkmate, singing pseudo-Indian songs and bonding with our girls.

***

In 1987 my Irish cousin Bernadette (also known as "Bernie," the one who sweetly played the accordion on my first visit to Ireland) announced her wedding and a honeymoon in Southern California with her new husband Pat. We were happy to welcome them for a few days for a trip that included a must-see visit to Disneyland. Worried about the hot California sun for these fair-skinned Celts, we provided an ample amount of sunscreen for Bernie and her spouse.

Disneyland always has long lines for rides, and this summer was no exception. Bernie slathered on the sunscreen. After a while her skin started to redden, so she repeated the application again and again.

"Joe was serious about this California sun," she said to Pat.

The redness only got worse. It took her about two hours to work out that she was allergic to the PABA enriched body lotion, but by then she looked like a boiled lobster. Sunburn would have been better. However, it was great to reconnect with my Irish family and to show them our hospitality, PABA included.

***

McCormack & Farrow was beginning to prosper. We landed a couple of divisions of Hughes Aircraft and several hospital clients. Jerry Farrow had a portfolio of high-tech companies, many of them in Orange County. The girls were healthy and enrolled in a nurturing pre-school called Broadacres, where we enjoyed an annual spaghetti dinner, cooked the previous day and reheated for compliant parents. It was served on toddler-size tables with miniature chairs for us adults. The things we do for our children.

Both girls were to go to Episcopal High School, their maternal grandfather's alma mater, in Alexandria, Virginia, where the problems for Anne would begin.

The storm clouds were beginning to gather, but for now, life was good.

Chapter 26

Count No Man Happy

"Count no man happy until the end is known."

—Solon

It seemed that I had achieved the American dream—a good marriage, two healthy children, a successful business and a comfortable home. I drove a navy-blue Porsche 911 Cabriolet, and I had a home office over the garage where I was able to work at times. My mother was in good health, and she was always willing to take the girls for a few days so Patty and I could travel.

I continued to go to AA meetings, prompted initially by the misery of my first California job in West Los Angeles. Patty was totally supportive of my time with my friends in the program. I had found a new sponsor who lived in a gate house of a larger home on the peninsula, running an upholstery business, a living salvaged from the alcoholic wreckage of his career as a publisher. The program was my bedrock and source of strength to meet our everyday challenges.

One day I got a call from my cherry-picking boyhood friend, Artie—now Arthur—asking if he could come for a visit. We spent an afternoon in deep conversation as we drove around the Palos Verdes peninsula, with its cliffs overlooking boulder-strewn beaches and crashing waves. We stopped at the Wayfarers Chapel, a stunning glass sanctuary designed by Lloyd Wright, son of Frank Lloyd Wright, tucked away in the lush cliffside woods high above the Pacific Ocean.

Arthur, my sensitive childhood pal, had been celibate since we were part of our neighborhood gang. He confessed to me that he had been sexually attracted to men his entire life, but he had never had the courage to act on it. I shared my coming out story with him, hoping to rekindle the friendship we'd had as children. Our mothers had kept in touch, but it's hard to renew a friendship that had lain dormant for so long. Less than a year later I received news of Arthur's death while he was student piloting a single engine Cessna 172 in the Tehachapi Mountains, 24 miles north of Lancaster. How much of life's joy he may have missed, I sadly reflected, by not being true to his feelings and acting on them.

I felt that my future was mapped out, and it seemed I would want for nothing.

Patty, Anne and Caroline at Camp Mystic in the Texas Hill Country.

***

Patty and I are sitting on a bench at the Portuguese Bend Club, a private seaside facility on the southern end of the Palos Verdes peninsula. Situated on a rocky beach, it's also a residential community of modest, one-time summer homes now occupied year-round, stretching up the hill to the gated entrance. The only light is from the moon and from the lamps lit in a dozen or more houses set well back from the beach. The smell of the sea and the sound of the surf are comforting. Patty wants to discuss her relationship with Clayton, her female college classmate and her romantic partner before we met. Clayton followed Patty from college to Houston, Houston to New York, and New York to Southern California. Patty asks my opinion, almost seeking, it seems, for a reason to maintain our marriage. I say that I don't envy how Clayton has been in constant pursuit of a commitment from Patty, tantalized at times and held at arm's length at others. I feel compelled to give this honest answer, and I feel oddly detached, as though this discussion has nothing to do with me. I sense that I am not making a very convincing case for myself.

***

The unlikely precipitating event was a broken sewer pipe. When we awoke one day, we found sewage in our semi-basement workout room, as well as bubbling up from the drains in the showers and tub. I was scheduled to leave on a business trip that week, a too frequent occurrence for an executive recruiter then. I took Patty and the girls to the Torrance Marriott until Patty could get a plumbing contractor to dig up our yard, replace the broken pipe and clean up the mess in the house. It was not a happy arrangement for her or for the girls. Meanwhile I was living in comfort at the University Club in New York.

Our best friends were Marty and Alex. We all liked each other, including their two children, who were the same age as ours. We took the train to San Diego to visit the zoo, and we frequently socialized together and with other couples in Palos Verdes. But there was trouble in Marty's and Alex's marriage. We suspected he had a mistress on the side, and how he made and spent his money as an attorney was something of a mystery. Not all of it was supporting his nuclear family. In any event, Marty was quite unhappy with things, and I can well imagine that she and Patty commiserated.

There was another factor in my opinion. I had long been comfortable with my sexuality, having dealt with any guilt or reservations about being bisexual. Patty, who had also had relationships with men and women, was in the process of coming out to a community of lesbians who were avid Virginia Slims Tennis Tournament fans. They included Clayton. I have always liked Clayton, and I didn't view her as a rival.

We went to marriage counseling, but for different reasons. I hoped to save the relationship, and Patty sought a graceful exit with minimal pain. Once the decision to end the marriage had been made, we took "reverse vows" at the behest of the therapist, acknowledging that the marriage was over. It was one of the most painful moments of my life.

***

On February 7, our marriage counselor Dave took us through the "divorce ceremony." I don't remember the exact words —something about making the best choice for us, thanking each other for the 10 years we lived together, etc. I didn't really hear the words at the time because I was remembering our marriage vows in the beautiful, stained-glass chapel of New York's St. Thomas's Church. There was a Juilliard string quartet playing a wedding march, the loving and smiling faces of family and friends, the recitation of vows with the parish rector Father John Andrew performing the ceremony. I could feel the hot tears streaming down my face.

I had 30 days to leave our house and find another place to live. We had to tell the children we were getting a divorce. Patty asked if we could say it was a mutual decision, but I couldn't find the will to say that. Letting Anne and Caroline know that I would be leaving soon was the most difficult thing I have ever done.

***

Anne and Caroline, who are 10 and 8, are sitting in their pajamas after dinner around the fireplace. Patty is managing the discussion, obviously thoughtfully rehearsed. Their reaction is shock and pain. I don't say much except to tell them it was a surprise to me too, but that I love and support their mother in her decision. What else can I possibly say? Caroline points out that Patty is the only one who isn't crying. I suspect she will do that later when she's alone.

It was the end of the marriage dream, but at least we were family and always would be.

I had a good friend in AA named Thomas R., who lived in Long Beach. I spent my first night away from home on his couch, my car packed to the top with my clothes, feeling as forlorn as a human being can feel at the loss of what I had expected to be my future. The lonely sound of a distant foghorn seemed a warning of the uncertainties ahead. Where will I live? Whom will I spend the balance of my life with? When will I see my children? How will we divide our property? How does this change my plans for retirement? Whom will we tell and when?

Chapter 27
In the Middle of Life's Journey

"Midway along the journey of our life/I woke to find myself in a dark wood, for I had wandered off from the straight path."
–Dante Alighieri

I am at an AA meeting in New York on one of my frequent business trips. I share about the divorce I am going through with a sympathetic audience. Seated across from me is a big middle-aged man in a full leather outfit, with numerous tattoos and piercings. The program attracts all types, but he is not someone I would normally strike up a conversation with. He comes up to me after the meeting. "I went through exactly what you're going through with the kids and all last year," he says. "I think I know how you feel. Here's my phone number. Call me if you want to talk."

I am dubious, but when I return home, I take him up on his offer. He sent me a book on surviving divorce which was passed on to him. He becomes my spiritual guide for the next few months. I learn that 80% of divorces are initiated by women in heterosexual marriages. The founding principle of AA is one suffering human being sharing with another in the same situation, and it works for divorce as well as for drinking. I'm reminded that angels sometimes come to us in the most unlikely disguise.

Approaching 50 and feeling the pangs of midlife, I found myself wandering in the proverbial "dark wood" of life's middle journey, as Dante once called it. To be sure, a wistfulness overtook me at times, but also the excitement of new possibilities.

The divorce, which was now largely about discussing joint custody arrangements and the sale of our Palos Verdes house, was as amicable as it could be. My feelings were still raw about ending our relationship, and sadness hit me like a tidal wave at times—at others it simply lapped around my feet.

It was time to find a path out of the dark wood.

***

My local AA pal and new Long Beach roommate Thomas R. and I decided to go to France using the accumulation of miles from my frequent business travel. Besides Paris, we visited the ancient cathedral of Chartres and the magical island of Mont Saint-Michel. I'd hoped this trip would clear my head, inspired by a *Washington Post* article about Jim Graham, a Washington, D.C. attorney. Jim, who had gone on a similar spiritual journey, returned to give up his law practice to lead the Whitman-Walker Clinic, the first HIV/AIDS service provider in the nation's capital. Seeking a similar epiphany, I prayed in Mont Saint-Michel Abbey for guidance.

Meanwhile, at McCormack & Farrow, Jerry and I were coming to an amicable business parting of the ways. We had recently completed a search for the American Foundation for AIDS Research (amfAR), the organization founded by Dr. Mathilda Krim and Elizabeth Taylor. It was the early '90s and the height of the AIDS epidemic. I was thrilled to work with an organization supportive of the gay community, a first for me. Like so many others, I had lost close friends and loved ones to AIDS.

Curiously, they were referred to us by the Robert W. Dingman Company, a search firm specializing in evangelical church searches and led by search pioneer Bob Dingman. Clearly, they were not a great match for amfAR, when AIDS was stigmatized as a "gay disease" and God's punishment for male promiscuity—at least in America. For me, it was a match made in heaven because I was able to come out professionally for the first time to a client and to combine my personal and professional interests in my work. I will always be grateful to Bob, a gentleman who lived his faith in Lincoln's words, "with malice toward none, with charity for all...."

With amfAR Chair and Founder Dr Mathilde Krim.

Announcing the formation of McCormack & Associates, I decided to come out publicly to build a practice that was personally meaningful and that would benefit my community. I had friends with HIV and friends who had died from AIDS. This was the only way I knew how to make my contribution. I was the first search consultant to come out in 1993. The story was picked up by the *Wall Street Journal*, the *Associated Press*, the *New York Times*, the *L.A. Business Journal* and numerous other AP subscriber newspapers, as well as internationally.

To quote Andy Warhol, "In the future, everyone will be famous for 15 minutes."

I had achieved my 15 minutes of fame.

The New York Times
Nathalie Weeks of Gay Men's Health Crisis, in New York, meets with Joseph McCormack, headhunter.
At Work/Barbara Presley Noble
The Unfolding of Gay Culture
An executive search firm for gay talent is just one example of a changing workplace.
THE WALL STREET JOURNAL.
YOUR CAREER MATTERS
A Gay Search Firm Finds a New Market
LOS ANGELES BUSINESS JOURNAL
New search firm specializes in recruiting gay execs for 'sexual orientation diversity'
ERN
THE INDEPENDENT NEWSLETTER OF EXECUTIVE SEARCH
50 LEADING RETAINED SEARCH FIRMS IN NORTH AMERICA
1997
EXECUTIVE RECRUITER NEWS
THE WALL
Employment Brief
Even Briefer
Search firm targets gay candidates
TIEMPO
Gays se mueven bien en mercados de EU
Agencia de empleos se especializa en su reclutamiento
Quiere Broadway conquistarlos

Chapter 28

Talking to Earthquakes

"We were different, sure, but isn't it precisely those gaps in which love, like a weed between the paving stones, blooms and thrives?"
—Pasha Malla

Here's the challenge: when you're on the cusp of 50, the options diminish. Either all the "good" men are already spoken for, or they're single due to some fatal relationship flaw yet to be discovered in protracted and agonizing heartbreak.

After dating a few men and women for a year, I answered an ad in *Frontiers*, the West Hollywood gay weekly distributed throughout the city. I don't remember the entire message, but it ended with "spiritual?" That immediately got my attention. We began a series of phone conversations that culminated in an agreement to meet for breakfast at Hugo's, a popular bistro on Santa Monica Boulevard and King's Road in West Hollywood. I entered the restaurant, prepared to be disappointed as I had been to several similar meetings, but I was happily surprised to see a tall and handsome blond stud smiling at me from a table near the front door.

The more we talk, the more down to earth and reasonable he seems.

"I'm not interested in the bar scene," says Gary. "I've just ended a relationship, and I'm looking for a long-term commitment." He had just started dating.

"He's surprisingly attractive," I think, which had not been my experience with similar meetings.

I was apparently one of several candidates to audition for Gary Hunter that morning because after an hour and a bowl of granola with apple juice, I was hustled along to make room for the next prospect. The granola with apple juice was an idea from my Long Beach roommate Thomas R., who was the food and beverage manager for the local Hilton. It was a bit like eating a bowl of sugar lumps with honey, and I learned afterward that it almost sank my chances with Gary. I've never eaten the combination again.

"So you moved here from upstate New York," I say. "Doesn't the prospect of earthquakes concern you?"

"No," he replies, "I talk to earthquakes as though they are a frightened or angry animal."

"What?' I ask, "Does it do any good?"

"I don't know," Gary replies, "but it makes me feel better."

I sense I am in the presence of an original thinker.

I felt as though I'd had a good audition, but I wasn't confident of a call-back. Soon after, I do get a phone call from Gary.

"Do you want to have dinner next weekend?" he asks.

Dinner is an upgrade from breakfast, and it usually lasts longer, so "yes," I reply.

We agree to meet at the Cheesecake Factory in Marina del Rey. After dinner, Gary asks, "Do you want to go back to my apartment?"

Without hesitation, I say, "Sure, that would be nice." And so began our 30-year relationship.

Gary had been in only one previous relationship—one that lasted 10 years, and he was temporarily single, so the timing was auspicious. At another time or in another place we would never have met.

Several weeks later, I took Gary to meet my children in the Ojai Valley north of Los Angeles, where their mother had bought a home, and it was an instant success. Later we stopped at Ojai's Krotona Institute of Theosophy, where Krishnamurti had renounced his role as their spiritual leader to follow his own path. There, in the peaceful sacred oak grove, I proposed to Gary.

My wedding to Gary Hunter September 2008.

Gary had attended Maharishi International University in Fairfield, Iowa, where he studied transcendental meditation, and we both had an interest in India and its spiritual traditions. We were to make three trips to the subcontinent, and I made a fourth to spend my month at the Amritapuri Ashram. We found that we both enjoyed international travel and made it a yearly event.

Over our 30 years together, Gary and I continued to share an interest in things spiritual, which proved to be the bedrock of our relationship. There were times when we meditated together and times when we prayed together. I like classical music and the theater; he likes contemporary music and sports of every variety. Unlike me, Gary is a natural athlete who excels at any sport he tries, including pickleball. He enjoys gardening and has cultivated a dozen or more mango trees of different varieties on our Palm Springs property. He is a student of Rancho Mirage Poet Laureate Dorothea Bisbas, and he has published several books of his poems.

"I hate musicals," said Gary. "It's unnatural for people to break into song in the middle of a conversation."

Ironically, he became a big fan of the television series *Glee*, where high school students and their teachers break into songs at the slightest pretext.

I like spicy food; he likes his food without spice (if you don't count salt and pepper).

"I don't like Mexican food," declared Gary, "because it's too spicy." Yet he loves quesadillas and makes his own nachos nearly every evening as a before-dinner snack.

Without musicals and jalapeño peppers, we began to build a life together in Los Angeles. But we needed to find a permanent home.

Chapter 29
Almost Under the Hollywood Sign

"Friends are the family we choose for ourselves."
–Edna Buchanan

After a year together in my Sycamore Avenue apartment, Gary and I decided to shop for a house. We found a small, but charming three-bedroom, two-bath cottage on Floyd Terrace, in a neighborhood called Hollywood Manor, offered at $230,000—a bargain, even in 1994. But after escrow closed, we learned that the previous owner, apparently a booze-loving cat lady, shared the home with over a dozen felines who'd left their indelible mark on every odor-absorbing surface in the home, a fact stealthily concealed by the realtor's 24/7 aromatic plug-ins. This necessitated the unexpected and unwelcome expense of replacing most of the hardwood floors and treating the subflooring.

On the bright side, the house had two working fireplaces and glass-paneled French doors that opened onto an enormous wooden deck. It was very light and airy and had undeniable charm.

Cleve Jones, the San Francisco ally of Harvey Milk and founder of the AIDS Quilt, once came to our new house in the Hollywood Hills, and he was surprised to find that Los Angeles wasn't an unending plain from the desert to the sea. We lived between Universal Studios and Lake Hollywood with a generous view of mountainous Griffith Park from the back deck. We weren't exactly under the Hollywood sign, but you could see it on a walk around Lake Hollywood across the street.

I was astonished to discover that the house opposite ours belonged to Jean Barrett and David Gibb—the same David Gibb I had met as an enlisted man stationed in Boston, the communications professional I had worked with at YPO in New York, the very same David Gibb my wife Patty and I had visited several years earlier upon our arrival in Los Angeles.

A mixed-race gay couple occupied the house next door on one side, and an elderly Holocaust survivor, Marta Frankel, lived on the other. Marta, in her 60s at the time, had retired as a bank teller.

Marta's malapropisms were always amusing: One of these days was "Once these days," Kibbles 'N Bits were "Kiblets," and Have a nice trip was "Have a nice drip."

More than a neighbor, Marta became a part of our family.

Chapter 30
The Viennese Collector

"There may be times when we are powerless to prevent injustice, but there must never be a time when we fail to protest."
–Elie Wiesel

If you were to open one of her two mirrored closets, you would find them tightly packed with an assortment of colorful women's clothing, many in plastic bags with the manufacturer's labels and price tags still on them, accumulated over several years of recreational shopping. Marta Frankel loved nothing more than lunch with a friend at Ca' del Sol or Prosecco's, followed by several hours in the Beverly Center looking for bargains at Macy's or Bloomingdale's. It was a collection of bargains successfully stalked and snared.

We met Marta when my husband Gary and I moved into the house next door on a quiet, tree-lined street in the Hollywood Hills. She was an active retiree after 40 years as a teller—and eventually head teller—at Hollywood State Bank, a local lender that merged and changed its name many times during her tenure. She was slender, about 5'4" and had fire-engine red hair — a color not found in nature, but identical to that of her friend Connie, both devoted patrons of the Toluca Lake hairdresser Paul Donnell. "I luf Paul," Marta would say. "He tells me everything that's going on in the neighborhood, and there's never any vaiting ven I make an appointment vit him."

We introduced ourselves shortly after we purchased our new home. Built like Marta's in 1939, the house, bright and cheerful with French doors in front and back, had a view across Barham Boulevard of the Griffth Park hills. Ninety years ago, houses in Los Angeles were built without compacting the soil, so there was the perpetual threat of land movement that had already eroded much of the back yard, replaced, in our case, with a spacious wooden deck. Marta's crumbling concrete terrace had several ominous cracks, which did not seem to alarm her.

We had recently adopted a lab mix named Amber from a local shelter. Marta loved dogs, and the serial installation of three dog doors from the back of our house, through the fence and into Marta's rear sunroom enabled us to share custody of Amber, who could choose her own happy place. Gary spent many an afternoon visiting with Marta and Amber, making small talk and listening to her repertory of stories, which she loved telling over and over.

"The only time I effer got a traffic ticket," she would tell us for the 20th time, "vas ven I turned to admire a handsome motorcycle policeman and I rolled through a shtop sign."

***

Marta came to the United States in 1941, her family victims of the Holocaust. Her father had managed the dining concessions for the Vienna Opera and the Vienna State Theater and several other entertainment venues. The family lived a comfortable upper middle-class life on Altgasse, one of the oldest streets in the city with a number of beautiful yellow stone buildings, close to Schönbrunn Palace and the Tiergarten, the city's zoo. Marta once showed us a photograph of her father, who had served as a loyal soldier in World War I, resplendent with his mustache in his military uniform.

In 1938, Hitler marched into Vienna with the Anschluss, annexing Austria to Nazi Germany. He was met by cheering crowds giving the Nazi salute, and the Frankels' troubles began. Karl Frankel's business was confiscated by the Reich, and the family was moved into a crowded apartment with four other families. Forced to wear the yellow *Judenstern*, they were further reduced to living in a single room with a communal bathroom. Karl Frankel had the foresight (and the money for a forged passport) to arrange passage for Marta to America in 1941, where she was to join her older sister, Tilde, who had preceded her two years earlier and settled in Los Angeles with an American husband. Marta's altered passport stated that she was 27, rather than 17. Later in life she could brag that she was 103, rather than 93. She never saw or heard from her mother or father again.

Marta, like most of us, was a bundle of contradictions. She was often warm, loving and generous, but she could also easily take offense at trivial matters, like failing to call her at an appointed time or unknowingly offending her until she was ready to explain the offense. Her list of offenders was long and ever-growing.

"Marta can be an injustice collector," volunteered David Gibb and Jean Barrett, who lived across the street. "If you get on her bad side, it can be weeks before she forgives you. And you may have to grovel."

Down the block lived Doris, another elderly Holocaust survivor, her number tattooed on her arm, from Poland. She and Marta were once friends, and Doris gave Marta a key to her house while she was away. Upon her return she asked for the key back, which ended their friendship, as far as Marta was concerned.

Marta's older sister Tilde, more a mother than sister to Marta, had a son named Roland. After Tilde's death from cancer, Roland was Marta's only living relative. Roland and his wife Rose—whom Marta never liked—were regular guests for holiday dinners at her home. One day Roland was driving home from Las Vegas when Marta was in bed with the flu. His route took him south on Barham Boulevard, a couple of blocks from our neighborhood. He neglected to stop in and check on her, and she never spoke to him again.

Marta was a beloved figure at the restaurants she frequented, nearly daily, for lunch. The wait staff found her sweet and caring, even though she never left more than a $10 tip, regardless of the size of the bill. We were often Marta's guests for lunches and dinners, and she would always say, "Order vatefer you vant," implying that the cost didn't matter. My husband and I frequently left an additional $10 or $20 on the table surreptitiously as we were leaving the restaurant, convinced our welcome would not be as warm as hers if we returned.

The love of Marta's life was Bill Reynolds, the owner of a very profitable auto dealership in Los Angeles, who became acquainted with her as her customer at Hollywood State Bank. Bill, a devout Catholic, was married to a mentally ill wife who had been institutionalized, and he did not believe in divorce. Hungry for companionship and intimacy, he was soon charmed by the perky teller where he banked, with fire engine red hair and an endearing Austrian accent. There could never be a marriage, of course, but he would fly her in his private airplane (she was terrified of flying) and drive her on weekends to Cabo San Lucas, where he had a seaside cabin. Soon after their relationship began, he gave her a frying pan for Christmas. She understood this as a test of whether she was a gold digger, so she raved about what a beautiful frying pan it was and gave him a bottle of his favorite scotch in return. The relationship lasted until his death, 20 years later.

Being more like a family member, I went to visit Marta when she was in bed after hip surgery. Seeing her disheveled and helpless, I was reminded of my mother, who also had an Austrian accent, and I burst into tears. I think that endeared me to her more than anything I could have said.

When Marta died many years later, I was her executor, and we arranged a memorial service for her at Mt. Sinai Cemetery, where she had purchased a crypt. There was a surprisingly large number of former co-workers, neighbors and friends in attendance. We set up a poster board with photographs of her and her family, and I made certain that the photos of her family were interred in her coffin. Like so many immigrants, she came to this country with a few photographs, little English and a dream.

Marta had two paintings, both of Vienna, by established artists. One was of the Schweizerhaus Prater beer garden and one of the Vienna Opera House. Marta's purchase receipt from the now defunct Robert Hecht Gallery valued them at over $6,000 apiece—no small amount for a bank teller a decade or two ago. An appraisal after her death however, priced them at only a few hundred dollars. Both have been donated to the Mizell Senior Center here in Palm Springs, where they may provide a moment of remembrance or pleasure to an elderly member.

Most of Marta's collections lost their value upon her death. But she touched the lives of many with her kindness, and those intangibles endure within the memories of those who knew her.

Chapter 31

Professional Growing Pains

*"Success is not final. Failure is not fatal.
It's the courage to continue that counts."*
—Winston Churchill

I am walking through Grand Central Station in New York late one evening on one of my frequent trips east. It's long past commuter hour, and a dozen or fewer people are heading to their last trains home or to the IRT subway. Grand Central Station is one of the most majestic interior spaces in New York City, dwarfing its few remaining travelers with its soaring arches and vaulted ceilings.

A few homeless people congregate in the waiting area until they are eventually rousted by the police. A shabby man begging for money is given a handful of pennies by a passerby. Enraged by the meager gift, he throws the pennies on the floor. When he leaves, I stoop to pick them up. I decide to be grateful for any gift from the universe, however small, for my fragile new business. Perhaps the difference between failure and success is the difference between grievance and gratitude. At least I like to think it's so.

***

Most people imagine that the attributes of a successful entrepreneur consist of vision, courage, and the *chutzpah* to take risks. And it goes without saying that passion is an essential part of that equation.

Equally important (although perhaps a bit less 'heroic'), the successful entrepreneur also demonstrates an aversion to authority, the arrogance to believe unwaveringly in a vision, and the social drive to better oneself and achieve. Necessity is frequently the decisive impetus.

What I learned at YPO is that truly successful entrepreneurs start businesses they understand from years of experience working in a similar field or sector. A retired postal worker who decides to open a gym or a restaurant might as well give his money to charity because it will be gone before he or she learns the business.

I knew how to do search. Jerry Farrow and I had built a successful practice from scratch. The scary part was whether I could succeed as an openly gay or bisexual search consultant in a society where 35 states still had sodomy laws on their books. One could be discharged from the military or fired from a government or private sector job because of sexual orientation. And there were 2.5 million documented cases of AIDS worldwide, the majority in the U.S. among gay men. Would I be ostracized or shunned by my professional colleagues or potential clients?

Well, it turns out the timing for my new business was good because there was a leadership niche begging to be filled, and most search consultants did not want the stigma of working with the organizations that became my first clients.

I opened McCormack & Associates in an executive suite on Figueroa Street in downtown Los Angeles. I had some money from the sale of our Palos Verdes house, and it took a year to begin building credibility in the HIV/AIDS sector and with the LGBT community. I began to build a unique national practice.

Some of the emerging AIDS organizations were getting significant government funding, and they needed capable leadership. Many, whose boards were populated by business executives and attorneys, turned to the largest executive search firms in the country for their recruitment. They were usually disappointed with the results. That provided me with an opportunity to demonstrate what a dedicated fellow member of the LGBT community could deliver.

I fell in love with amfAR and Dr. Mathilde Krim. She was a biomedical researcher, a philanthropist, a socialite (her husband Arthur Krim was the Chairman of Orion Pictures and United Artists), and a humanitarian. In 1983, she and others founded the AIDS Medical Foundation in New York, which merged in 1985 with the National AIDS Research Foundation in Los Angeles, established with a gift from Rock Hudson and Chaired by Elizabeth Taylor. I completed many senior staff searches for the newly formed American Foundation for AIDS Research (amfAR) over my first two years in business. When we conducted an Executive Director search, our two final candidates were Bella Abzug's daughter Liz Abzug and Whitman-Walker President Jim Graham.

In the final selection process, I drove Jim to Elizabeth Taylor's home in Bel Air for her approval to lead amfAR. Her home surprised me. Modest by movie-star standards, it was nonetheless filled with violet geodes (her color) and artwork, a Matisse and Chagall among them. She was then married to Larry Fortensky, a construction worker and her eighth husband. We imagined he was watching our approach up the graveled driveway through the kitchen screen door. Greeted by one of Elizabeth's assistants, we were made comfortable and awaited her arrival, carefully coifed, and dressed as you would expect from a star of Hollywood's golden period. She was gracious and insisted on being called Elizabeth rather than Ms. Taylor. The conversation flowed easily, and she appeared to like Jim Graham.

Shortly after that meeting, however, Jim's candidacy was sabotaged by several amfAR staff members who feared he would be too authoritarian for their taste. To this day, I believe amfAR lost someone who would have been a great leader—one who was the inspiration for my trip to France to seek my vocation.

Elizabeth made a generous contribution, however, to the Whitman-Walker Clinic after our meeting that enabled the organization to build the Elizabeth Taylor Medical Center at 1701 14th Street in Washington, D.C.

***

Several years later, Jim Graham retired from Whitman-Walker, and McCormack & Associates was retained to recruit his successor as executive director. The Whitman-Walker Board of Directors was assembled by Jim from an assortment of D.C. power brokers and major donors, many of whom didn't much like each other. I had no idea what a buzz saw I was walking into.

When we were down to two final candidates, we had a board member and significant donor who had applied for the job and an African American public health department executive who ran the AIDS ward at L.A. County Hospital. Identifying and presenting candidates of color was imperative. Nearly every major AIDS organization was run in the 1980s by white men and women. As the disease continued to have a disproportionate impact on communities of color, especially those with limited access to healthcare, everyone recognized the need to have that segment of the population included in leadership.

The board divided into two factions: one for the major donor and one for our Los Angeles candidate. Naturally, I lobbied for the Los Angeles candidate as the one with more appropriate management experience and one who was representative of the diversity and inclusion goal of our search. The defeated faction resigned from the board when we announced our selection, and they immediately began opposition research on our new executive director.

Some digging into public records revealed that he had been arrested and charged with a couple misdemeanors for sexual solicitation in Griffith Park. This would not have shown up on our due diligence background checks because only felonies are listed. It would have been illegal under California law, in any case, to deny someone employment for misdemeanor infractions. There were also some unsubstantiated allegations of sexual harassment by co-workers that had not been revealed in our reference checking.

The faction opposed to our hire persuaded the Board of Directors to fire our candidate. The Chair of the Search Committee called me, "We expect you to return our fee," he said.

"We will re-do the search at no additional fee to you, but unless you can return our time, we aren't offering a refund," I replied.

Could we have been more thorough in our reference checks? That's always a postmortem consideration. I would likely still have supported his candidacy because of his dedication to the work and the contribution he could have made to Whitman-Walker, but the board members and staff members who set out to sabotage him succeeded and destroyed the career of a good and caring man.

I contacted our errors and omissions insurer and filed a complete report with documentation of our work. The board eventually dropped their threat to take legal action. With a story about the fiasco soon after in D.C.'s gay newspaper, the *Washington Blade*, this was the low point of my career as a recruiter. Two Washington, D.C. friends stood by me in my lowest hour: Wayne Shields, the CEO of the Association of Reproductive Health Professionals, and Bob Witeck, a partner in the D.C. public relations firm of Witeck & Combs. I am grateful for these friends who continued to believe in my work.

I had come to realize that recruiting in the HIV/AIDS community was far more complex than simply identifying good candidates. Politics, personal rivalries, and sabotage were part of the underbelly of the great and noble work being done by the best and most dedicated leaders. I would have to learn to be a political strategist as well as a recruiter. I also realized that I would have to expand my business focus beyond HIV/AIDS and the LGBTQ community, which led to many new adventures.

Chapter 32
Loyalty & Betrayal

"Honesty pays, buy it don't seem to pay enough to suit a lot of people."
–Kin Hubbard

Executive search can be difficult, frustrating, and occasionally nasty when politics are involved. The joys are meeting extraordinary people who are changing the world with their vision and talent and the satisfaction of seeing an organization thrive and prosper because of the talent we bring to it.

Over nearly 30 years, our practice broadened to include progressive nonprofit organizations of all kinds, including the ACLU, Amnesty International, Planned Parenthood, the Natural Resources Defense Council, as well as several colleges and universities. I found I had a knack for business development, which included extensive advance preparation, energy, and enthusiasm in a presentation. I strove to connect an organization's mission to my own lived experience.

When we were in competition with others for the executive director position at the Los Angeles Homeless Services Authority (LAHSA), we walked the downtown homeless encampment streets and visited the newly built respite center that provided showers, lockers, haircuts and six-hour cots for the homeless.

"We spent yesterday on Skid Row," we said in our presentation to the LAHSA Board of Directors, half appointed by the mayor and half by the County Board of Supervisors.

"We also visited your new respite center, which could be a model for similar sites throughout the county. Your work is an inspiration, and we can find you an inspirational leader."

That preparation became a template for our successful business development efforts.

As the business grew, I was blessed with several intelligent, motivated, and memorable administrative assistants who were essential to my success—and one who was a costly lesson.

After the first year, I abandoned my expensive and unnecessary downtown office. I set up an operation in one of the downstairs bedrooms facing the back of the house, and we soon installed two other work-stations—one for my administrative assistant and one for my spouse Gary. He managed the books, the invoices and the accounts payable. That was our team for many years, occasionally saying good-bye to one administrative assistant and hiring another.

Justin Akin was my first assistant. He had worked for and been a client of AIDS Project Los Angeles, and he was great at his job. After a couple of years, he went on to a responsible position at UCLA.

A second assistant was Shawn Simpson, whom we hired from responses to a help wanted ad. Shawn had been the executive director of a very small AIDS support organization in the Midwest. The organization had gone out of business, and he headed west.

Shawn worked for us for about four years, and he was skilled at all the necessary software, at scheduling and at contracting with researchers for candidate generation. Shawn was dealing with some AIDS-related health issues. When he went to the hospital, he insisted on taking his personal computer with him and continuing his work from a hospital bed, which I thought was unnecessarily heroic. He often worked long hours without being asked.

Unfortunately, he was also stealing money by setting up false accounts with mailbox addresses and billing us for research that never happened. We passed some of these expenses on to our clients, to whom I later made restitution. I came to learn that this devotion to duty is sometimes the hallmark of an embezzler, like the accountant who never takes a vacation.

Shawn and his partner decided to buy a house in Orange County, and he insisted he could continue his work from there. I was dubious, but willing to give it a try. When I began receiving invoices for $5,000 or more for research, I decided we needed to track down the vendors.

"Why are we suddenly paying so much for research?" I asked Gary. I had signed off on invoices for lesser amounts for some time without question. "Have you verified some of these charges?"

"I'm not sure," replied Gary," but I'm certain these are legitimate expenses. I can't believe Shawn is dishonest. He's such a hard worker."

I decided to do my own checking, and I found that many of the "vendors" were merely a postal box at *Pack and Send*, each at a different location. Gary had become friendly with Shawn and his partner, so he refused at first to believe my suspicions until I showed him the incontrovertible evidence.

We contemplated turning Shawn in to the law, but because we had sometimes paid him "off the books," we were vulnerable if he chose to turn the tables and alert the tax authorities. We decided instead to sue him for the $120,000 we could document that he had siphoned out of the business over 3-4 years. On a friend's recommendation, we hired a lawyer at a major law firm in Century City.

At $600 per hour, our legal bills mounted quickly. As an attorney friend once said, "How much justice can you afford?" After filmed depositions, Shawn and his partner were unable to mount a credible defense. We reached a settlement for $60,000, with a judgment to be filed against them for that amount. In the end, our legal bills totaled about $60,000, and we were only able to collect $25,000 several years later—and that was after Shawn died from AIDS-related complications. So, we were out about $155,000 and should probably have been satisfied with

Until the End is Known

simply firing Shawn and eating the initial loss.

It's a lesson I haven't forgotten.

***

The exceptional assistant with whom I worked for 10 years was Justin Warren, who was a runner-up for a similar position as Assistant to the Executive Director with The Point Foundation. I was lucky to get him in 2006, when Gary and I had settled in our Hollywood Hills home and the business was flourishing. Justin was a graduate of DePauw University in Indiana with previous experience in customer service at Toyota. As the first point of contact for our business, this experience was an important qualifier.

My first impression of this bespeckled but handsome young man was his beaming smile and engaging warmth. And he was tall! His computer skills were first-rate, his telephone manner courteous, and his efficiency of the highest caliber. Our first business trip together was to Denver, where we took a briefing from the LGBT Center of Colorado, beginning a search for an executive director. Justin and I took several trips after that, but most of our time was in my home office, where he and Gary became friends as well. At the time, Justin had a relationship with a professional event manager, and both lived in Silver Lake.

Because Justin was eager to learn and soon took on the responsibilities of a search consultant. I tried to familiarize him with all aspects of executive search, and we made a great team. During the 2007-2008 real estate collapse and subsequent recession, our business slowed to a trickle. I continued to pay Justin and promised him a generous bonus. I also offered to make him a partner if he would stay with our business until the end of the year. When an employee is too valuable to lose, it's smart to provide the incentive to stay, sometimes referred to as the "golden handcuffs."

A few years later Justin and his then significant other drifted apart. Before long, on a return trip to the Midwest, Justin met a man named John with whom he wanted to share the rest of his life.

"I'm going to move to Columbus," said Justin.

"This is a surprise," I said, chagrined and disappointed because I had viewed Justin as my successor. "Are you sure this is what you want to do? Let's both give it some thought."

"I'm not sure this would work remotely," I concluded. "Our clients are nearly all in New York, Los Angeles, Chicago or Washington, D.C. Columbus is not a business focus for us. I'll be sorry to lose you, but I guess you need to follow your heart."

Justin soon found his footing in Ohio and continued working in corporate talent acquisition with L Brands and other major companies, a role for which he is perfectly suited. He credits me with being a good mentor. I credit him for helping me build our business and for being a loyal friend, growing from Administrative Assistant to Partner. I had the opportunity to visit Justin and John in the cozy and charming house they soon bought in more affordable Columbus and meet their dog, Ollie. It was the quintessential happy family. I consider helping Justin grow into the successful professional he is as one of the most important accomplishments of my business career. In the end, the impact we have on others' lives may be our most important legacy.

Another kind of legacy from a good friend was about to change my life.

Chapter 33

Red Devil Tools Fights AIDS

"It's bad enough that people are dying of AIDS, but no one should die of ignorance."
—Elizabeth Taylor

In the 1950s George Ludlow Lee, the son-in-law of the founder, became the Chairman of Red Devil Tools, Inc., a manufacturer of caulking, glazing, sealants and other products for construction. In 1979, I met John Lee, his son, at an AA meeting in New York, where we became friends. The family princeling, John, was attractive, bright, and talented—and unfortunately an alcoholic. We were more acquaintances than good friends, but we became re-acquainted when we both relocated to Los Angeles and continued to see each other at AA meetings in West Hollywood, our relationship deepening into a friendship.

John began having health issues because of his HIV status sometime in the late '90s. No longer able to work full-time in advertising as he had in New York, John settled into a quiet life with his modest, but welcoming house in West Hollywood with his dog Charlie.

One day in 1995, John suggested having an in-home AA meeting on Tuesdays with a few close friends in the program, and the round-robin gathering became one of my regular nights out. The meeting was usually followed by a dinner at the French Market or another local bistro. With Scott L., Jack R., Carlos P., Eduardo S., Bill H. and Bob D. we typically had 8–10 participants, which gave everyone an opportunity to share.

After a couple of serious health crises, John was conscious of the need to plan for his death. He asked me if I would be the executor of his estate, and he asked Scott L. if he would care for Charlie. Having played the same role for my mother and aunt, I had a good idea of what was required of an executor, so I agreed.

John had an inheritance from his father, as well as his house in West Hollywood, so there was no small sum of money that needed to be managed. We identified the Tides Foundation in San Francisco as a reputable place to establish a donor-advised fund. Tides managed the investment portfolio and the tax reporting, and I was given authority to distribute the income on behalf of the John Lee Fund to AIDS and LGBT service providers, as well as similar social justice, policy, and social service organizations.

My management of this largess was a boon to my developing business, as I could now make generous donations to organizations who were struggling to provide services to people with AIDS and who were advocating for LGBT equality. It was my privilege to honor John's wishes over the next 20 years until we had spent down the fund.

Gary's and my relationship flourished because we each had outside interests as well as interests in common. These friends in AA were my support group. Gary had friends who pre-dated our relationship, as well as the friends we made as a couple.

Gary and I began to build some financial security for our retirement, but we were to make some serious mistakes.

It's a story that begins in a small Kurdish Village in Turkey.

Chapter 34

Icarus Takes Off from Kurdistan

"A small profit is better than a big loss."
−Ron Rash

Afran Barzani heard the school bell ring on a Saturday afternoon as he drove his family's goats from their pasture into their pen in the small Kurdish village of Bashmaq, little more than a collection of mudbrick houses with thatched roofs surrounding a central courtyard. Situated in the Taurus mountains near the Turkish and Iraqi border, Bashmaq boasted a one-room schoolhouse, where the students could learn about Turkish history and culture, as well as receive Turkish and English language instruction.

Curious about a summons to school on a typical vacation day, Afran walked the quarter-mile to the cinderblock schoolhouse, a "gift" from the Turkish government to the poor farming community, which only a generation ago, was part of the Kurdish independence movement brutally suppressed by the government in Ankara.

"Students," the teacher addressed the assembly in Kurdish, "This is Mr. Sanders from America. He represents the American Field Service, which provides a one-year stay with an American host family. He's here to ask for volunteers for this program. Those of you who have had at least two years of English language instruction are eligible."

Afran was the top student in his class, but he had never dreamt such a thing was possible. *"Amerika!"* he thought. He had only seen pictures of this fabled land in a geography book. "I need to ask my father, but I would like to go!"

Two weeks later, a letter came to the Barzani family. Afran, his two brothers and a sister, gathered around the kitchen table of their two-room house. "Congratulations!" it said in English with a Kurdish translation. "You have been selected by AFS to spend a year at an American high school with the Deegan Family in Hershey, Pennsylvania."

***

The Deegans were to become more than a one-year host family for Afran. Joe Deegan, a senior engineering executive at Westinghouse, and his wife Sarah had three children of their own, and they readily welcomed this bright and promising immigrant into their home. Afran — now "Frank" to his new family and friends — had to learn to eat with a fork and knife and to undress in the locker room for P.E., overcoming his cultural taboo about nudity. He also had to be encouraged to take a shower more than once a week. But he soon took eagerly to American life.

When he graduated from high school, the Deegans sponsored his education at Penn State University, where he graduated with a degree in engineering.

After college, Frank took a job with Lockheed Martin in Los Angeles, which brought him to California as the real estate boom of the 1980's was beginning to accelerate. Frank began to wonder if there was more opportunity for an ambitious person in real estate development than in the design and production of bombs.

When he had earned enough money, Frank brought his brothers and sister to America. Brother Kareem Barzani seethed with resentment against the Turkish government, which had denied the Kurds their own homeland for over a hundred years. While Frank was becoming an entrepreneur, Kareem was organizing protests in Washington, D.C., where he camped out for several months in Logan Circle decrying Turkish oppression.

Frank sympathized, but he wanted to realize the American prosperity dream before becoming an activist.

***

One day, attending an open house for a Santa Monica apartment building on the market, Frank met my future husband Gary. "You know, I've been thinking about buying a building like this, rehabbing it and converting it to condos," said Frank. "Would you be interested in investing? I think the return could be significant."

Gary had inherited a modest sum of money from a grandparent, so he was open to the idea. "Frank is a real go getter," later said Gary to me. I was dubious, but impressed when a year later, Gary's return was four times his investment. "Count me in on the next project," I said.

Meeting Frank for the first time, I was impressed by his energy. Frank was neatly dressed in carefully creased trousers and a freshly ironed shirt. Olive skinned and slightly built, he had a hawk-like gaze that belied his ready smile and cordial manners.

"How did you choose "Frank" as your new name?" I asked.

"I wanted a name that sounded American, but not very interesting," he answered with a laugh.

Our early investments were all in Santa Monica, where beach-adjacent properties were in high demand, and Frank soon had four or five limited liability companies, buying sometimes derelict apartment buildings and converting them to luxury condominiums. It seemed like the sky was the limit.

Frank was a part-time Kurdish activist in support of his brother, returning regularly to his family home in Turkey, where he was known as "The General." He had business documents identifying him as the "General Partner" in our limited liability corporations (LLCs) formed for the construction projects. We imagined him in an elaborate uniform, with epaulets, resplendent with medals as he returned to his native village, no longer a goatherd.

Within a few years, Frank had over 50 projects under construction from Santa Barbara to Riverside County, each an independent LLC. And he had attracted over 40 investors, all eager for a share in this real estate money machine. They included Mei and Li Yeung, a mother and daughter from Shanghai, Basam Saleh, a Palestinian resident of Jordan, Ivan Bartek, a Czech construction manager from Prague, the Deegan Family in Pittsburgh, and Judge Roy Kaufman, a prominent civil rights attorney and Administrative Court Judge in Los Angeles, who taught law at UCLA.

Frank enlisted Judge Kaufman to visit Abdullah Ocalan, the leader of the PKK, the Kurdish resistance movement in Damascus. The PKK were considered terrorists by the Turkish and U.S. governments. As the saying goes, "One man's terrorist, is another man's freedom fighter." Judge Kaufman, who had by now invested in several of Frank's projects, agreed to draft a constitution for the putative government of Kurdistan.

Some of us began to worry that Frank might be over-extended, using equity from one building to borrow money to purchase a new property before any profit was realized. But motivated partly by greed, we kept rolling our returns over from one project to the next until we had over $3 million invested—all equity on paper, of course.

Frank's Chief Operating Officer quit one day, and he began sharing his serious concerns with us and our fellow investors. Gary and I, loyal to Frank, initially ignored these reports as the rant of a disgruntled employee. But it gradually became clear to us that Frank *was* over-extended, with so many properties and outstanding construction loans. Whatever skills he may have had as an engineer, he lacked as a construction manager and as a businessman, hiring workers on-the-fly to complete various phases of construction and importing expensive "finishes" from China that sometimes were the wrong size or didn't meet U.S. code requirements.

Frank convened a meeting of the investors on a sultry August day at his spacious modern office on Donald Douglas Loop at Santa Monica Airport, where he kept a four-seater private plane.

"Starting new projects every month concerns us," worried one of the investors.

"And if you are co-mingling funds from one LLC with another it's illegal," shared another.

Frank dismissed our apprehensions, but there were storm clouds on the horizon in 2007, as the real estate boom was on the verge of collapse. The great mortgage default began, and rumors of an impending recession had us worried. Frank continued to juggle too many competing priorities as his ambition outran his capacity to manage it all.

Under considerable pressure from the lenders, as well as the investors, Frank decided his family needed a break, and they made plans to fly to Clear Lake in Humboldt County for a Labor Day camping trip. Frank had purchased a single engine Aurora four-seater airplane, which he flew regularly from Santa Monica to his new home in Carmel Valley. He had received 760 hours of single-engine pilot training and qualified for his pilot's license in 2003. But he had not taken the plane manufacturer's recommended training program.

The plane was loaded with six passengers, including the children, and was 85 pounds overweight. The air was unusually hot and thinner at the Humboldt County airport's altitude. Missing the runway on his first approach, Frank banked for a return landing, but there was insufficient lift or speed for success. It crashed nose down, instantly killing all aboard.

As Frank was the primary loan guarantor on each of our projects, the banks soon moved in to foreclose on the construction loans, wiping out the equity of the private investors. It was the perfect storm and the end of our real estate speculation.

"Well, I guess we'll have to re-think our retirement plans," said Gary after several fruitless attempts to negotiate with the lenders.

"We still have a successful business," I replied. "It hurts, but we'll survive."

Only one property on Olympic Boulevard was near completion, and Gary and I managed to salvage a little over $100,000 from those condo sales. It was a catastrophe with a tragic ending for our friend. However, we were still young enough to rebuild—unlike some others who lost their retirement savings.

And so ended the flight of our dreams and those of the goatherd from Bashmaq, whose grand ambitions proved his spectacular downfall.

***

Gary and I spent most weekends in Palm Springs, where we had bought a second home, sometimes departing from L.A. on Thursday and returning on Monday morning. We had always intended to retire to the desert. We were tired of the traffic gridlock in Los Angeles and the many disadvantages of city life. Our financial losses made it increasingly untenable to maintain two houses, so the decision to become full-time desert residents was an easy one.

Coping with our financial losses, we sold our Los Angeles house for $600,000 to Brigitte Nielsen, a model, actress and TV personality, once married to Sylvester Stallone. We moved full-time to Palm Springs, where I continued to run my business from home—long before the COVID pandemic made it a commonly accepted practice.

Surviving these financial reverses was stressful enough, but family issues were soon to add to our problems.

Chapter 35

A Very Good Life

"He was still too young to know that the heart's memory eliminates the bad and magnifies the good, and that thanks to this artifice we manage to endure the burden of the past."
—Gabriel Garcia Marquez

I took my mother, 78 years old, to the oncologist's office after a routine physical showed a lump in her breast, something she claimed had been there a long time. He recommended immediate surgery followed by radiation and chemotherapy—the full, brutal battery of our primitive treatments for cancer. She might have lived much longer with what I now suspect was a slow-growing tumor, but surgeons always speak with authority that is seldom challenged by their patients. She held my hand when we got the diagnosis and recommended treatment, something she hadn't done since I was a very small boy.

She had surgery, radiation, and chemotherapy, followed by a daily regimen of Tamoxifen, an estrogen blocker that is supposed to prevent the recurrence of breast cancer. Mom immediately began suffering from fluid retention in her arm nearest the mastectomy, as her lymph nodes appeared to be working overtime. Soon she began developing abdominal pain and received a diagnosis of ovarian cancer—a potential side effect of Tamoxifen. From there, it was a steady decline with more and more medical complications, including surgery to "debulk" the tumor in her abdomen. She began losing significant amounts of weight and was unable to regain it.

If I take a lesson from this experience, it's to challenge a doctor's diagnosis and recommended treatment if my instincts tell me it doesn't make sense. There are worse things than dying from a slow growing tumor, and one of them is dying from overly aggressive medical intervention.

During the following months, I traveled almost biweekly from Los Angeles to San Jose to spend time with mom, and I was supported by my two sisters, Elizabeth, who lived closer to her, and Marianne, who flew down from Eureka, near the Oregon border. Even with my siblings' support, this was a stressful time, as anyone who has cared for a parent in the end stages of their life understands.

One day, we knew the time had come for mom to prepare for her death. We arranged for a priest from the local Catholic Church to give her last rites. More than a dozen family and friends gathered around her single bed in the bedroom she had slept in for 32 years. My mother, like most of us, was a "Christmas and Easter Catholic." But the last rites, which were so incredibly moving, gave her some peace, as we individually told her how much we loved her. It brought home to me the enormous power of ritual.

A week or so later, I returned for a visit, and she asked me to prepare a massive dose of the morphine she had been prescribed for pain with some apple sauce, so she could finally end her suffering in a dignified way.

"Mom, are you sure you want to do this?" I asked.

"I'm very sure," she replied.

We sat and talked for a long time until she began to get very sleepy.

"I've had a good life," were some of her last words to me.

This seemed a remarkable statement from someone who had left home at 23, never to see her parents again, borne a child out-of-wedlock, lost two husbands to early deaths, lived with spousal alcoholism and abuse, and raised an autistic child.

I suppose what matters in the end are the blessings we enjoyed and the happy times we can remember.

Not long after, she slipped into a coma. I returned to Los Angeles, expecting to hear that she had passed away, but my sister Marianne informed me that she had revived, extremely annoyed that she was still alive. A compassionate doctor prescribed more morphine, enough to relieve her suffering and complete her transition. A few days later, her body began to shut down, and one night she died in her sleep.

***

Gary called me to the phone in the afternoon a few days later, and I learned that my mother had taken her last breath. I had been so busy being a part-time caretaker, managing the details of her estate and preparing for her memorial service, that I was numb to the emotional impact of her loss until that moment, when a flood of childhood and lifetime memories and the finality of never seeing her again hit me like a train.

I remembered the delicious Austrian apple slices, cherry pies and vanilla *kipferl* (shortbread cookies) awaiting me whenever I returned from college or the Navy. I remembered her offering to send me the airfare from her meager savings to come home from New York on my first traumatic visit. I remembered her pride at my wedding to Patty and how she loved to dance with me and our guests. I hadn't anticipated the suddenness and depth of my grief, but I had Gary to comfort me as I wept, as I have since offered to comfort him upon his mother's death.

I traveled to San Jose for the memorial service where I delivered the eulogy. The night of the service, my sisters Elizabeth and Marianne and I were gathered at the dining room table, exchanging stories about our mother. It was then that I had an out-of-body experience. Suddenly, I was removed from the scene, observing the three of us in our grief. I felt *"this is how it is meant to be. All is well and will be well."* It was a transcendent experience of acceptance and peace.

My sense of peace gave me the strength to deliver mom's eulogy, which went well. But, on some level, I was still grieving, and I confess that I broke up when reading certain passages that I've excerpted here:

> Cecelia Swisher's name never appeared in The New York Times. She was never given an honorary degree by a college or university. She was never nominated for one of George Bush's Point of Light awards. She was, however, a genuine American hero: a woman whose self-sacrifice for her loved ones—and especially her children—set her apart from the norm and set an example of unselfish service for all of us in the room today.
>
> As a child I didn't understand or appreciate how weary she must have been or how much of a struggle it was to clothe and feed us and to keep us off of public assistance. Once, during a particularly difficult period, she did apply for welfare for a couple of months. When she had the money, she insisted on repaying it to the Department of Social Services because her pride would not allow her to accept a hand-out. This must have confused them terribly, since no one had ever offered repayment before.
>
> My mother always made me feel special. Her faith in me gave me the confidence to get a scholarship and attend college, to get into Officer Candidate School in the Navy, to start and build a career in New York, to marry a woman like my ex-wife Patty and to father my two beautiful daughters Anne and Caroline. I don't think any man can be successful unless the first and most important relationship in his life—that with his mother—is a good one.

***

Two years later, I was to deliver a similar eulogy for my sister Elizabeth. She was diagnosed with fibroid tumors of the uterus, treatable if found early. But she refused entreaties from her Kaiser Plan doctors to have a hysterectomy, even though she was long past child-bearing age. She opted instead for "natural" remedies, not the decision that her children or I would have made. Whether these decisions were a result of our mother's experience with modern medicine I never knew. During the worst of our stepfather's drinking, she was always my protector. After she left to get married, I often spent time with her, her husband Phil and baby Jeff, later joined by additional children Jenny and Annette.

When I was in the Navy and during the years I lived in New York, I could always count on the occasional letter with photos of home from Liz. The letter was usually written in a circular fashion in the margins, upside down and every which way. The photos were often the back of someone's head or of their feet, but it was the kindness of the gesture and the time she took to remember me that mattered. Liz could always be counted on to express an opinion on any topic. Usually, it was based upon the last article she'd read in *Ladies Home Journal* or the *National Enquirer*. It often made for a lively conversation at the dinner table. Sometimes I found her ideas odd, if not downright goofy. She was convinced, for example, that her ex-husband, Phil Curry, somehow had ownership of Camp Curry in the Yosemite Valley.

And when it came to those family dinners, Liz always supplied something delicious from the oven. At one time, I think she had 64 cheesecake recipes in her inventory. She worked hard all her life, from her first job as a teenager at the EGGO potato chip plant in San Jose to the many years she put in with children at a daycare center. I can never remember her being unkind or harmful to anyone. Hers was a sweet and generous nature.

I was soon to learn more about the challenges of parenting myself.

Chapter 36
Success in Public & Trouble in the Family

"Don't let what you can't do stop you from doing what you can do."
–John Wooden

When our daughter Anne was 10 years old, she broke her arm on the school playground. The summer of that year, she did not go to Camp Mystic in the Texas Hill Country with her sister and cousins. Instead, she and I took a trip to New York, where we stayed at the University Club. We visited all the tourist sites and had pizza at Patsy's on East 60th Street, followed by a tram ride to Roosevelt Island and dessert at Serendipity, an iconic ice cream store since the 1960s. It's one of my happiest memories of Anne and one of the last before her troubles began.

By the time the girls reached adolescence, Patty and I were divorced, and they were living in Ojai where they attended middle school. I had them on alternate weekends and on alternate holidays.

After some discussion, Patty and I decided to send first Anne, then her younger sister Caroline, to Episcopal High School (EHS) in Alexandria, Virginia. It was their maternal grandfather's alma mater, and it had gone co-ed a few years earlier.

In retrospect, I think the age of 14 is too early to leave home. Aware of the widespread drug problem in California's schools, I assumed a boarding school would be a safer place for young girls, and I knew they would get a good education.

The first year, Anne did well academically. However, she was a stranger to the southern society of mean girls and the jock/bro culture of boys at Episcopal. I know there were many students who found other groups at the school, but Anne was pretty and smart, and she so wanted to fit in with the "cool" kids. She began to adopt their values and behavior. We noticed some changes in her behavior early, and she began taking prescription amphetamines like Adderall, prescribed for the very fashionable disease of attention deficit disorder. The girls who had the prescriptions sold them to the girls who didn't, until they could get their own. Soon she was getting in trouble for breaking curfew and for unauthorized absences from campus. We were 2,567 miles away, so we were unaware of much that was going on.

Like many adolescent girls, Anne suffered from an eating disorder. This was tied, of course, to her use of amphetamines to control her appetite. It would take a separate chapter to enumerate and describe the treatment programs we provided for Anne, from residential eating disorder programs to wilderness therapy for teens to inpatient and outpatient substance abuse rehabilitation. While she sometimes seemed to cooperate with the therapy, she always relapsed once out of the program—if she even completed it.

We found out years later that Anne had been sexually assaulted by a member of the EHS football team at a party where she went as someone's date as a freshman. This is something she never shared with us or anyone at the school at the time. We also found out years later from her younger sister, the only person she had confided in, that Anne had been molested by a male cousin a couple of years older when she was a pre-adolescent. If we had only been aware of these events at the time they occurred, we might have been able to address the trauma or minimize the damage.

On the surface, things seemed normal, and we attributed Anne's rebellious behavior to the typical growth pains of adolescence and puberty. Whenever I was in Washington, D.C. on business, I would stop at Episcopal to take Anne out to dinner and have a visit. We talked about boys, her teachers, and the family, but never about those feelings of low self-esteem and undeserved guilt that must have tortured her most.

When Anne returned home for summer vacation one year, her mother and I were shocked to hear her say disparaging things about gay people. Her mother and I were both in same sex relationships at the time. Until that moment, Anne had acclimated to that. This homophobic reversal concerned us. I decided to raise the issue with Episcopal High School, and the new Headmaster, who had recently succeeded a 30-year predecessor.

"You have a problem of homophobia here," I said, meeting with him in his office. Also in attendance were the Dean of Students and a student counselor.

"I know we do," he replied. "But I'm not sure how to deal with it."

At the recommendation of friends, I suggested that Episcopal invite Kevin Jennings, the founder of the Gay, Lesbian and Straight Education Network (GLSEN) to campus. GLSEN was the first organization of its kind in the country's secondary schools. Kevin, the son of a North Carolina preacher, had started an organization to keep LGBTQ students safe from the bullying and discrimination he experienced as a student.

Kevin is one of the most gifted orators of our generation, and that is not hyperbole. EHS called for an all-campus assembly, which was boycotted by a handful of students whose parents accused the school of promoting homosexuality. By the end of the assembly, Kevin received a standing ovation. Anne walked up to him and asked if he knew me.

"Your dad put me up to this," he said with a smile.

Kevin's appearance was the beginning of greater tolerance and inclusion on the EHS campus. And I think Anne was proud of me. At least she later said so. I understand that the Latin teacher came out shortly thereafter, and the school formed a campus gay-straight alliance. Similar groups now exist at over 3700 schools nationally.

Daughters Anne and Caroline.

Soon after, I joined the Board of Directors of GLSEN, Kevin's organization, and I was proud to support his important work in high schools throughout the country.

Meanwhile, Anne's grades and behavior continued to deteriorate.

As the co-parent for our daughters, Gary suffered through some of Anne's worst behavior. He was more the disciplinarian than I was, not that setting boundaries did anything to tame two rebellious teenagers. As difficult as those years were, he never faltered in his support for me, and that has made all the difference.

We received annual holiday letters from friends describing their perfect families, with happy and successful children, citing their numerous achievements and blissful matches. I was aware that we were reading a semi-fictional narrative, but I sometimes felt I had fallen short as a father. Anne's misbehavior had been the focus of too much of my attention, and I needed to be a better parent to our other daughter Caroline.

Chapter 37

Two Mothers and Two Fathers

*"All happy families are alike;
each unhappy family is unhappy in its own way."*
–Leo Tolstoy

Our younger daughter Caroline was born almost two years after Anne in Torrance, California. She went to Broadacres, the same preschool as Anne and to the same elementary and middle schools in Ojai. We also enrolled her at Episcopal High School when she was 14.

I think Caroline always had a stronger sense of self and more self-esteem than Anne. At Episcopal, she dated an African American boy for a while, which was a shocker for many of those southern belles from small-town Dixie. I loved her defiance of these pernicious norms.

Caroline followed in Anne's footsteps for a while, but she asked to return home for high school, and we honored her wishes. I think all adolescents have adjustment problems, and it's easy in our society to get caught up in the drug culture. Caroline was struggling too, but her mother was able to find an outstanding adolescent therapist for her named Zev. It proved to be life changing. Would it have helped Anne? We don't really know because he didn't feel he could take two siblings as patients, and Anne had gone back to EHS after a rocky third year.

I often ask myself if my divorce from Patty set into motion some of the personal struggles of our two daughters. The fact that Patty and I were in same-sex relationships was undoubtedly a challenge for our adolescent children in the 1990's before gay marriage was even on the horizon. We learned that from the notions Anne brought home from her boarding school.

Anne graduated from Episcopal High School in a haze of alcohol and cocaine, and she enrolled at UC Santa Barbara, where she failed to complete her first year. After entering an eating disorder program, she decided to attend Kansas State University, for no better reason than a suggestion from her recovery roommate. Manhattan, Kansas, in the geographic center of the country and far from the coastal cities, seemed like a safer environment to us. Anne attended AA for a while, enough to graduate from K State. Patty and I flew out to Kansas for the event, and Anne again was drunk and high, disappearing halfway through our celebration dinner.

***

After home schooling for part of her education, Caroline was accepted by the University of California at San Diego, one of UC's most desirable campuses. She dated several young men, including a Brazilian named Rafael. We always liked Caroline's choices of romantic partners because they were responsible, good people.

Rafael still had to complete college in São Paolo, and his U.S. visa was limited, so she strongly considered following him back to Brazil, even flying south to meet his family. It wasn't to be for many reasons, including timing. Both needed to finish their education in their home countries before thinking about marriage.

They parted ways sorrowfully, but there's more to the story nearly 10 years later.

Not long after, Caroline met a sailor in San Diego, and they began dating. Nathan was a Petty Officer, a rescue swimmer and a candidate for the Navy SEALS. He was conservative, polite and responsible. Nathan was transferred from San Diego to Norfolk, Virginia, about the time that Caroline decided to move to Richmond, where Patty and Clayton had relocated across country to buy a home. Soon Nathan was commuting from Norfolk to Richmond to spend weekends and time off with Caroline. One day, he asked me (as I had asked George Neff 24 years earlier) for our daughter's hand in marriage. I don't know if that's still a custom, but it certainly charmed me. They had a beautiful black-tie wedding at an Episcopal Church in Richmond, followed by a reception at the historic Jefferson Hotel. I gave the bride away and served as an emcee of sorts for the reception. Patty graciously ceded the role to me as Caroline's father, and I was honored to do it.

I brought two young men with me: Justin Warren, my talented business colleague, and Kevin Ferenchak, a pre-med Point Scholar from Chicago. At the time I was on the Board of Directors of the Point Foundation, the LGBTQ scholarship fund, and I had taken a personal interest in Kevin's success. Both handsome young men were welcomed by the Richmond gay establishment, many of whom were at the wedding.

Caroline's sister Anne was not invited to the wedding. By now, she had been in numerous recovery programs for eating disorders and drug and alcohol addiction in urban, rural and wilderness settings, none of which had altered her downward trajectory. For long periods of time, we didn't know where she was, but she had chosen a life that didn't include her family.

Caroline and Nathan had three children over the next 10 years: Olivia, Henry and George. All were blond, blue-eyed beauties. Henry appeared to be a slow learner until we figured out that he needed glasses. It takes a while to stand up and walk if you can't see well.

Gary and I have spent Christmas with Patty, Clayton and our grandchildren nearly every year since Olivia was born, and we enjoy being grandparents. Patty has always loved Christmas, and it's inevitably a big production with seasonal decorations throughout the house and gifts piled high under an enormous Christmas tree. Anne and Caroline grew up with two mothers and two fathers, and our grandchildren consider it perfectly natural. I suppose it's a cliché, but there is comfort in knowing that some part of me will live on in the next generation and thereafter when I'm long gone.

Nathan struggled with SEALS training, not because he wasn't extremely motivated and fit, but because he had significant injuries from the vigorous and punishing regimen. When Nathan decided to leave the Navy, he enrolled at Virginia Commonwealth University to complete his undergraduate degree. He excelled in school and was admitted to the Arabic Studies Program at Georgetown University. He also won a Fulbright Fellowship that enabled him to live for a year in Jordan, where he became fluent in the vernacular. He once described speaking University Arabic in public the equivalent of speaking Shakespearean English to the hot dog vendor at Yankee Stadium.

After Jordan, Nathan got a job training military personnel from Arabic-speaking countries in weapons use, with weapons provided by the U.S. Government. This included spending weeks at a time or longer in the Middle East. His absences from home, like mine a generation earlier, did not contribute to harmonious family relationships. And when you hang out with ex-military weapons trainers, politics tend to skew ultra-conservative.

Caroline decided to separate from Nathan, which saddened me, but my loyalty had always been and must be to my daughter. Her happiness was the most important consideration for me. I talked openly with Nathan about Patty's and my divorce. While it's clear in retrospect what some of the reasons were, there was no merit in pointing fingers or trying to assess blame. Good and loving people sometimes grow apart. It was essential to protect the children from any conflict or hostility because co-parenting is a life-long responsibility whether you are married or divorced, and whether you have one father or two.

After a suitable period of time, Caroline got back in touch with Rafael from Brazil, who had returned to the U.S. to work, and they rekindled their college romance. I was able to walk her down the aisle for a second time at the Greenbrier Hotel &

Resort in West Virginia, where her mother has a home. F. Scott Fitzgerald famously wrote, "There are no second acts in American lives," but Caroline and Rafael have proven that wrong.

I would soon have an unexpected opportunity to be a father to some remarkable young men. Would there now be a second act in my future?

Chapter 38
What's the Point?

"The mediocre teacher tells. The good teacher explains. The superior teacher demonstrates. The great teacher inspires."
—William Arthur Ward

In 2001, Bruce Lindstrom and his spouse Carl Strickland established The Point Foundation, the first scholarship fund for exceptional LGBTQ youngsters, often marginalized by their families or communities. In 2002, when I was serving on the GLSEN board, Bruce called me to set up a meeting and discuss hiring the first Executive Director for the new enterprise.

The day Bruce and Carl came to our Los Angeles home to discuss the search, the house was undergoing a roof replacement. The hammering sounded like a flock of frenzied woodpeckers trying to topple a tree.

"You're going to offer scholarships to LGBT students?" I asked.

"What did you say?" replied Bruce.

"Scholarships!" I replied.

"And mentoring," said Bruce.

"Dismembering?" I queried.

"Mentoring, mentoring, like a coach or guidance counselor," replied Bruce.

Bruce suggested we share a weekend at their timber and glass-clad home on Lake Tahoe. There we could talk surrounded by a view of mountains, billowing clouds, and the glorious sheen of the lake at sunset. Inspired by our surroundings, I saw an opportunity to help get an exciting new organization off the ground and soon joined his evolving board. Bruce and Carl had three houses on a choice piece of real estate jutting out like a peninsula into the lake. Hence the name of the Point Foundation.

The guest house was as large as the main house, filled with California realist art, offering a panoramic view of the lake, and equipped with temperature, sound, and window shade electronics that required a tablet-sized screen to manage. The shower had a steam-bath feature. At least our Hollywood house had a new roof.

Like many start-ups, Bruce's directors were colleagues and personal friends. Some were experienced nonprofit board members, and some were not. John Pence, who owned a nationally known and successful art gallery on Post Street in San Francisco, was a tremendous asset. I quickly realized that the foundation needed experienced LGBTQ community leaders on its board to provide steady governance, financial support, and credibility. We went about finding these folks, some of whom I knew from my work for the previous eight years in the AIDS and LGBTQ sectors. In addition to the governing board, we also established a Board of Advisors, marquee names who led other significant organizations, but who could lend their prestige to Point. Among these were Chuck Middleton, the President of Roosevelt University, Lorri Jean, the long-time Executive Director of the Los Angeles Gay & Lesbian Center, and other prominent LGBTQ leaders.

Bruce and Carl were extremely generous with their time and money, but we had to leverage this financial support many times over to make a significant impact in the LGBTQ community. And we did. In addition to scholarships, the Point Foundation matched a mentor with each of its scholars. Often, this proved more impactful than a check for tuition.

Our second class of scholars included Justin Kidd, now the father of two adopted boys with his husband Rob, and a justice of the peace in Oregon; J.R. Mortimer, now an artist and freelance writer in Connecticut; Zach Zyskowski, a television production

Joseph A. McCormack

executive in California; Jacob Weldon, who has established a philanthropy career in Texas; and Kevin Ferenchak, a practicing ophthalmologist in Georgia. All were young and many struggling when we met and interviewed them, and all are now successful in their chosen careers.

Interviewing scholarship applicants, we heard many heart-rending stories of family rejection. One college sophomore told us about how his parents intervened in high school when he was coming out. He had grown close to a teacher who acknowledged his own sexuality to counsel the young man. The parents threatened the school and demanded the teacher be fired. They then sent their son to a therapist to "fix" him. Never having shared this story before, the applicant broke down and was unable to continue the interview. He wasn't selected that year for a scholarship. I spoke to him after the interviews and encouraged him to apply again the following year. He did and was awarded the funds he needed to complete college without the support of his parents. He is now a successful professional. Like several of our scholars, he has excelled in every way.

As Point grew, Judith Light, famous for her role in the TV show "Who's Boss," and her manager, the late Herb Hamsher, joined the board. This opened the door to support from other entertainment celebrities, and we also began to cultivate support from major corporations committed to diversity and inclusion, among them, Disney, Wells Fargo, and Motorola to name a few.

In the last decade, Point has awarded more than $47 million in scholarships and leadership training to students of every race, ethnicity, gender, and gender expression. In 2021 alone, Point offered scholarship assistance to 389 students from the community college level to graduate school. Nearly all have excelled academically and have shown leadership potential. Each was paired with an adult advisor and coach. I served as a mentor to several of these young people, with whom I have remained friends. I remained on the governing board for six years. I was the first Chair of the Board of Trustees, community supporters united in their engagement with Point. Under the able leadership of Jorge Valencia, Point has continued to grow and prosper.

In a summer address to the Point Scholars at an annual leadership conference, I offered the following, which I had learned from AA:

"To establish intimacy with a friend or a mentee, I must be willing to share my vulnerability, my mistakes, my insecurities and my shortcomings. Our abilities and accomplishments are obvious. We are all high achievers, or we wouldn't be here. A good mentor is not simply an authority figure. To build that heart connection, it requires openness and trust. Once that trust is established, there is nothing we can't achieve together. This is the great secret of mentoring."

Helping Bruce, Carl and John Pence build the Point Foundation has been the most rewarding volunteer work of my life because I see the impact that its financial and emotional support has had on the lives of so many deserving young people. We haven't saved the world, but, like the starfish thrown back into the sea, we've made a difference that counts for those we've touched. By modeling the lives of successful LGBTQ people, I hope we have inspired some of them. My ongoing relationship with the Point Scholars I've known and mentored has enriched my life, a welcome addition to my biological children.

Chapter 39

The First Time I Retired

> "To other countries I may go as a tourist,
> but to India I come as a pilgrim."
> –Martin Luther King, Jr.

In 2018, I decided it was time to retire. We had enough invested to pay our monthly expenses, we had no mortgage, car payments or credit card debt, so Gary and I concluded that we could live modestly on our social security and monthly investment income.

A few years earlier I had brought Michelle Kristel into the business, and she was now the Managing Partner of our newly named McCormack + Kristel. A former client when she was the Executive Director of "In the Life," a public TV documentary series on the LGBTQ community, Michelle had invited me to lunch one day at *Robert*, a ninth-floor restaurant overlooking Central Park on Columbus Circle. The green 843-acre rectangle stretched out below us. Our lunchtime conversation turned into a nine-year working relationship that was mutually profitable and always amicable. Michelle was more than capable of succeeding me as the leader of McCormack + Kristel. It's comforting to know that the business is in capable hands and will live on.

I had long thought about spending some time at an ashram in India. After three visits to the subcontinent, I still had a fascination and affection for this exotic and spiritually advanced (to my mind) country.

Recollecting the first time Gary and I traveled to India around 1995, I felt a kinship with the country—almost a déjà vu experience—as we deplaned and navigated around the cows freely wandering outside the New Delhi Airport. The city, enveloped in a perpetual fog of smoke and industrial pollution, was nonetheless a riot of scents, colors, and sounds, so very unlike western cities in my experience.

Me at the Amritapuri Ashram In Kerala, India, 2020.

Our first visit followed the usual tourist routes to the Taj Mahal, Rajasthan, Varanasi and Udaipur, but we also made a side trip north to Rishi Kesh, a corner of northern India made famous by the Beatles and other spiritual seekers. With ashrams located on either side of the pine forest-lined Ganges, flowing out of the snowpack in the Himalayas, Rishi Kesh is so much cleaner and more appealing than many of the densely populated urban areas further south. The hotel we stayed at was a half-step above a hostel, with a bed on the floor and a bathroom with an open shower. I remember the night watchman patrolling the streets, beating his stick on the pavement and blowing a whistle periodically to assure everyone he was on the job. It may have provided comfort to the local residents, but it continually woke me out of a sound sleep.

A highlight of our trip was the visit to Benares (now Varanasi), spiritual center of the Hindu faith and nearby Sarnath, where the Buddha was said to teach his disciples and where he ended his days.

We embark on a small boat onto the Ganges before dawn and watch as the residents of Varanasi come down to the ghats or piers on the Ganges, where they ritually bathe in the sacred river, practice their yoga and burn their deceased on the funeral pyres. It remains one of my most vivid memories of India and one of the most impressive sites anywhere in the world. With no visible signs of modernity, we could have been watching similar rituals a thousand years ago or more. It is, perhaps, the moment I fell in love with India.

***

On the boat to Udaipur's Lake Palace Hotel, we met two Americans who had recently visited Bombay (now Mumbai) and who told us about an Indian AIDS activist named Ashok Row Kavi. He had established the Humsafar Trust, the country's first men's sexual health organization focused on the prevention of HIV infection. Gay men and lesbians in India were still very much in the closet in this deeply conservative society (thanks to England's Victorian laws), so many gay men sought anonymous sex at night in public spaces. Ashok and his team distributed HIV prevention literature to this population, as well as to sex workers, which included India's unique Hijra population, transsexual men who presented as women and who often had little access to education or healthcare.

In subsequent years, we made two more trips to India, which included Mumbai and the resort beaches of Goa. India's former Portuguese colony, Goa was a clean white-sand beach south of Mumbai, lined with resort hotels. Everywhere there were remnants of Portuguese rule, including the *Basilica de Bom Jesus*, built in 1615 and containing a relic of St. Francis Xavier, a co-founder of the Jesuits and a prolific missionary to India, the Malay Archipelago and Japan.

We began our second visit with a stop in Mumbai and an introduction to Ashok, and I offered to support his work in whatever way I could. Ashok later traveled to the United States as our guest. We introduced him to Sandy Thurman, who was, at the time, the national AIDS advisor to the White House. Over high tea at Washington's Mayfair Hotel, Ashok shared his history as a journalist, gay activist and AIDS service provider. Sandy was able to get a $100,000 grant from USAID for Ashok's work, which put the Humsafar Trust on the Maharashtra State regional map. In Los Angeles, Ashok attended an all-employee assembly at the L.A. Gay & Lesbian Center, where he shared about his life and work to an eager audience. Finally, he appeared on a panel at the annual Creating Change Conference sponsored by the National Gay & Lesbian Task Force.

Gary and I were avid international travelers. Each year, around the holidays, we would plan an overseas excursion, using the many frequent flyer miles I accrued from my business travel. At this point, we have traveled to every continent except for Antarctica.

On our third trip to India, we again visited Ashok, then hired a boat to sail through Kerala's inland waterways, where we ate the daily catch and slept on deck under the stars—a dreamlike interlude in our journey. We also took a side trip to Madras (now Chennai) on the southeast Indian coast, where we visited the Theosophy Center. Established by Annie Besant and the Theosophy movement at the turn of the century, it was where Krishnamurti was selected and groomed to be a world spiritual leader. Since my marriage proposal to Gary in the Sacred Grove in Ojai, where Krishnamurti taught for many years, I had always wanted to visit the mother house of Theosophy in India.

We also visited Sri Lanka, the island nation off the coast of Tamil Nadu, staying at the magnificent old colonial Galle Face hotel. The hotel was built on the water, and we could hear the surf crashing continuously from our room. We hired a driver to take us into Kandy and the Temple of the Tooth in the Sri Lankan mountains and to the elephant orphanage, where we met young elephants of all sizes and playfulness. It's probably not a good idea to get too feisty with them because even a young elephant can weigh 300 pounds or more.

Our stop at a roadside restaurant on the way back to Colombo proved to be a mistake. With only intermittent electricity, the refrigeration of their food was problematic. We paid dearly for the experience for a couple of days, not knowing every 30 minutes which end to point toward the toilet.

India was a country I loved for its spirituality and its many exotic features. It seemed like the logical place to go for a period of contemplation and reflection.

At the urging of Jazzmyn, my long-time friend, AA sponsor and life coach, I began making plans to spend a month at the Amritapuri Ashram in Kerala, situated on the southwestern coast of India on the Arabian Sea.

My romance with India wasn't over yet.

Chapter 40
Darshans & Dish Towels

"Selfless execution of duties with equanimity, serenity, without attachment to fruits, is the spirit of karma yoga."
—*Bhagavad Gita*

A car and driver meet me at the regional airport in Trivandrum, a palm tree-laden tropical town of one- and two-story buildings on the Arabian Sea. Although it's a February morning, it's already warm and humid. The driver who picks me up thoughtfully brings some homemade samosas prepared by his wife. When we finish our breakfast, he throws the styrofoam containers out of the car window, where they land on the side of the road. A hundred years ago, most litter would have naturally decomposed. Today, plastic trash is all but a permanent fixture of the countryside. A culture dedicated to transcendent spirituality is oblivious to the garbage it creates all around us.

Although the ashram is less than 70 miles from the airport, it's a four-hour journey on increasingly rural and sometimes poorly maintained two-lane roads, often stopped for livestock and women in colorful saris returning, baskets filled with fruit and vegetables, from market. Something unusual about India is that there are abandoned houses right next to newly constructed ones. It seems that no one has any use for them or their construction materials once the residents are gone.

The driver has a cousin in Cincinnati and asks if I might know him.

***

Amritapuri was established by the followers of Mata Amritanandamayi Devi, or Amma, as she is more popularly known. A rare female monastic, she is known for hugging people rather than preaching a specific doctrine. Newcomers are offered darshan, or an audience, with Amma shortly after arrival, when I get my first of two hugs from her. She answers questions from her devotees during the evening bhajans, which are songs and prayers, but she only speaks Malayalam, which requires a translator. Malayalam, the dominant regional language, sounds like someone narrating an exciting soccer game with a mouthful of hot mashed potatoes.

I describe the ashram as a campus because it resembled a college campus more than the stereotypical ashram with simple one-story buildings, a temple and modest living arrangements. This ashram is home to more than 3,500 monastic disciples and householders. Here there were multi-story dormitories, as well as circular cottages for families, a large dining hall, also used for assemblies and ceremonies, the obligatory temple, dedicated in this case to the divine mother Lalita Devi or Kali, whose 1,000 names are chanted daily by her female devotees. It also features an Indian café with upscale vegetarian food, a western café, where omelets, pancakes and cappuccinos are served and an ice cream stand, open in the evenings after dinner.

Offerings included meditations twice daily on the carefully cleaned beach, classes in the Bhagavad Gita, the Upanishads and other Hindu scriptural classics, yoga classes, ayurvedic astrology and a pharmacy, early morning pujas (devotional ceremonies), nightly singing and chanting in the great hall and silent retreats for those who wanted them. There was an excellent library containing books in English and other languages on every spiritual practice imaginable.

I was assigned a single room over the western style café, which proved to be a surprisingly quiet location. There was no air conditioning—unneeded in the winter months of my visit—only a large overhead fan. I had a toilet, a sink and a bucket and tap for a shower. As we were in the tropics, the tap water was always warm, so showers (in the style of the ice bucket challenge) were not unpleasant. Each resident is encouraged to volunteer a couple of hours a day in service. I was assigned to the drying station for midday and evening meals. Everyone washed their own dishes in communal sinks, but they had to be dried before storage. That was my job, usually working with one assistant, and I did it with joy and enthusiasm. The assistants came and went. A girl from the French West Indies named Clarice taught me that a dish towel is a "torchon," while a bath towel, like a napkin, is a "serviette." It might come in handy if I can't pay my bill in a French restaurant.

Visitors to the ashram came from many countries, but the majority were from the U.K. and western Europe, including France, Germany and Italy. We also had groups from China, Japan and the occasional Russian. The Americans here were typically upper middle class young women from Boston or Darien, or middle-aged women who are divorced or widowed and seeking new meaning in their lives. Occasionally, they were bossy.

"Make a straight line for the coffee," barks one. "We have a lot of people to feed this morning."

Some young travelers, passing through, were just backpackers from many countries. Wearing white was encouraged for those serious about their spiritual quest.

On my third day, assembling at the central temple, I befriend Paul Jones, a 27-year-old yoga teacher from Liverpool. Tall, lean and dark-haired, he has a ready smile. Paul and I meet for a meal almost every day, take many long walks along the beach and have deep spiritual discussions.

"If God is good," Paul asks, "how do we explain the poverty and suffering all around us?"

"God is neither good nor bad," I reply. "We imagine God in our own image and attribute human characteristics, including gender, to the creator of all that is. If there is a God, it is either the sum totality of everything or nothing."

"Then why try to be good or moral?" asks Paul.

"That's a question posed by Dostoevsky in The Brothers Karamazov," I reply, "as well as by many other great thinkers. It's also a theme of the Bhagavad Gita."

We find a restaurant down the road from the ashram where they serve chicken tandoori and other non-vegetarian fare and make it a Sunday night routine. Paul is gentle and eager to learn. He has an accent like John Lennon, a fellow "Scouser," as they call people from that region of Britain. At 27, Paul has traveled a lot. He's worked in bars and restaurants, been an au pair in Italy, and he's an accomplished ballroom dancer. He is fascinated by olive-skinned girls. There is no shortage of them in India.

Paul would strike up a conversation with anyone, and he had no judgment about others. There was a boyish innocence about him, and he had a curious and open mind. He would tell you anything about himself, and he brought lightness and kindness and joy to every conversation. You would have to be a stone not to love him.

I find that I have lots of time on my hands, a new experience for me, and it takes a while to slow my western-style pace. I go for runs in the morning at about 6 am on the road along the beach. After my bucket shower and a 20-minute meditation, I have eggs and toast or a pancake in the café beneath my room. I quickly learn to cover my food if I leave it for a moment to get water or coffee because the ubiquitous monkeys are eager to make off with whatever they can snatch and carry.

I attend guided meditations almost daily with Amma and evening meditations as a group on the beach, listening to the gentle surf of the Arabian Sea and feeling the warmth of late day sun.

My friend Paul decides to move on to another ashram where they emphasize hatha yoga. A group of us meet for breakfast before his 9:30 departure. The group includes a Slovenian, four devotees from China and a girl from Toulouse. We have some laughs, and when it's time for Paul to leave, we each hug him, and one of the Chinese breaks into *Auld Lange Syne*. He doesn't know the words, but he hums the tune. As Paul walks away, he doesn't look back. I don't think he wants us to see the tears in his eyes. We keep in touch through Facebook.

I attend pujas, or devotional services with a Brahmin priest at 5 am. Silver-haired, dressed in white, he chants the ritual Sanskrit devotions, burning sandalwood scented incense during the 90-minute ceremony. I make offerings for the safety and health of my older daughter suffering from addiction. In my second brief audience with Amma, I show her a photo of Anne and, through a translator, ask her to pray for Anne's recovery. It may be my imagination, but she appears alarmed when she sees the photo—not the favorable or comforting reaction I'd hoped for. Does she intuit something about Anne's future?

***

I learned there are many paths to enlightenment, but the three principal ones are *karma* (path of duties), *jnana* (path of knowledge), and *bhakti* (path of devotion). It became clear to me that my path was—and always had been—the path of duties or positive action in the world.

To quote spiritual teacher David Levine, "For a long time I took more than I gave…where once I looked at people for what I could get from them, I now looked at them for what they might need. The opening of the heart, a karma yoga, is the reversal of grasping." It was the very essence of my vocation as a recruiter for AIDS and LGBTQ organizations.

And 2018 still wasn't the time for me to retire.

Chapter 41
Ashes to Ashes

"They shall not grow old, as we that are left grow old."
—Laurence Binyon

Said Bob McK., looking at my photo, "Jeff didn't look anything like that when he died." Jeff had succumbed to AIDS five years before. I received a phone call from one of Jeff's friends with the news.

I was carrying a photograph of Jeff Lowell, my first love in college, dressed in a crew neck sweater, with his bright blue eyes and chestnut hair in a classic preppy cut. Bob was carrying a simple black urn containing Jeff's ashes.

Bob and I trudged slowly up the dirt path on a bluff overlooking the Pacific in Palos Verdes on a beautiful sunny day. Dust devils swirled in the breeze, and the gravel scrunched underfoot as we climbed to the summit, with a few white cumulus clouds in the distance and a vista as far as the eye could see. The rolling surf crashed far below us, a mix of deep, resonant rumbles and soft, whispering sighs.

I remembered the deep arguments and discussions Jeff and I had in college over a bottle of wine, sometimes long into the night. I also recalled his excellent cooking, his quiet laugh, and the tenderness of his touch on a rainy Berkeley afternoon, when the world seemed full of endless possibilities.

I recalled the day Jeff returned from the Peace Corps in Malawi to stay with me for a few days in my New York apartment.

He had contracted malaria in Africa and was only beginning to regain some of the weight he'd lost. While I was at work, a friend offered to take him to the boat show at the New York Colosseum, which proved to be a cultural shock to someone who had lived for two years in a village without indoor plumbing. To Jeff, the money spent on luxury yachts could have fed thousands of people in the impoverished villages he'd known.

Jeff and I had kept in touch during his time in the Peace Corps and long afterward when he bought a house in Oakland, earning a master's degree and taking a job with the California Medical Association, where he worked for over 25 years. Like me, he had come to terms with his addiction to alcohol in his mid-thirties and joined Alcoholics Anonymous, which further strengthened the bond between us.

I asked Jeff's friend when she called to let me know when and where they were having the memorial service, but I never heard from her again. I thought about Jeff often during those five years, regretting the fact that I'd never had the opportunity to say a proper goodbye.

By chance, I met Bob McK. in a Palm Springs AA meeting. He had retired to the desert from a teaching career in Oakland. I asked him if he had known Jeff from AA meetings in the Bay Area. "Know him? I was his AA sponsor and friend for over 15 years," he replied. "In fact, I have his ashes, and I haven't quite known what to do with them."

And so, Bob and I planned our seaside journey to scatter the ashes of our friend in a place he would have loved. When we reached the summit, Bob opened the urn, and we each gently scooped out a handful of ashes.

Jeff was an atheist, so a prayer didn't seem appropriate, but we paused for a moment of memory and sober contemplation. It was a proper farewell, as I whispered goodbye.

As we launched the remains, a sudden gust of wind blew them back in our faces. "I guess we've both breathed in a bit of Jeff today," I laughed.

"I know he didn't look like the photo at the end," I said. "But I will always see him as the boy I met in college 50 years ago."

The funerals and memorials continue as time and age take their toll.

Chapter 42
Ashes to Ashes, Part 2

"We are things of a day. What are we? What are we not?
The shadow of a dream is man, no more."
–Pindar, 518–438 B.C.E.

Will's estate instructions were very clear: he wanted his ashes scattered off the coast in the Pacific Ocean.

As his executor, I chartered a boat, arranged for a caterer and a bartender for the excursion and the memorial for his friends and family, and we set sail on a sunny, but windy autumn day from Marina del Rey. The air was fresh and salty, the waves catching the light and reflecting it back in a dazzling display. The vastness of the sea inspired me to reflect on the transience and limitations of one man's life.

Will had lived in both Silver Lake and Palm Springs for 30 years. He had lost a partner of many years to AIDS and had been a solitary soul for some time. He and my husband Gary met on a tennis court and became real estate investment partners and fast friends. Eventually, Will became a friend of mine too. Because his family lived in North Carolina, Will asked me to be the executor of his living trust, which was complicated with numerous assets and many beneficiaries. The boat trip was the least complicated instruction.

Will had owned a four-unit building in Silver Lake with rental income from three of the apartments. His top floor apartment had a large rear deck with a stunning view of downtown Los Angeles. His household included Spiff, a rescue dog who occasionally fell off the deck into the bushes below and a parrot named Harriet, whom Will later discovered was a male.

"The parrot flew into my screen door one day, and I picked him up, stunned from the impact. I couldn't tell whether he was a boy or a girl, so I named him after my mother because he never stops talking," said Will.

Will had spent a career working for the City of Los Angeles Department of Transportation. You can see his designs on virtually every freeway on-ramp and off-ramp in Los Angeles County. "I love to drive nowhere in particular on the freeways to admire my work," he explained.

One New Year's weekend, Will invited us to Palm Springs, where the temperature was 80 degrees and the sun shone on a breathtaking canvas of azure blue sky, hardly a cloud in sight. We were hooked, and soon made an offer on a condo in the Palm Springs Racquet Club, selling at bargain prices in 1994.

After we later sold our Hollywood Hills house, we sometimes stayed in Silver Lake with Will on our trips into the city. Will had an architect design a wall unit that opened into a Murphy bed in his spare bedroom, but he decided at the last minute to scrap these plans and buy an auto-inflating double air mattress. It had a slow leak, so when we slept on it, we gradually rolled to the center of the bed, nearly on top of one-another.

Will drove an ancient Mercedes with about 200,000 miles on the odometer. He ordered a room full of Mexican furniture for his home, which appeared designed to drive Americans to orthopedic clinics in Tijuana. Will, who had a substantial estate, was frugal to a fault. His drinking had steadily increased since his retirement, and he refused to eat in a restaurant that didn't have a liquor license. As we usually split the bill, we were often saddled with an extra twenty or thirty dollars for his martinis and wine.

"Will," I said, "we are happy to split the cost of dinner with you, but we don't think it's fair to pay for half of your liquor." After some discussion, he agreed, and our dinners together became less expensive and less frequent.

At one time, Will was a regular tennis player, and he belonged to a gym, but as his drinking increased, he put on a substantial amount of weight. He never appeared drunk, but I'm not sure he was ever entirely sober either. We suspected that cocktail hour began earlier and earlier for him.

Will had a small circle of friends, including Annika and Britta, two Swedish sisters next door. For reasons still obscure to me, he had a falling out with them, and their neighborly visits stopped. It likely started as a misunderstanding that grew into a grudge, as pride on both sides prevented a reconciliation.

Will had a living trust that he had planned to amend to include new beneficiaries and delete some of the old, but somehow, he never got around to it before he died of a sudden heart attack in his home one afternoon. So Annika and Britta, Will's long-ago tennis coach Walter, and a fired one-eyed handyman named Fred each came into a generous inheritance, much to their surprise. We inherited the parrot.

***

As the boat left the marina, the captain said, "By law we need to be two miles off the coast before we can scatter human remains. It's choppy today, so I'd advise staying inside until we get to the drop-off point."

Choppy was an understatement, as the boat rolled, pitched and yawed in the waves as we made our way west. In one roll, the bottles on the bar came crashing to the deck. "Can't we get closer to shore where the ocean isn't so rough?" I asked.

"Well, I'm not supposed to do this, but I'll take her further in," said the captain, by now off the coast of Manhattan Beach.

Will's sister Sandy had the urn with his ashes. Twist as she might, she could not get the top unsealed. She grunted and grimaced, her face turning red with the effort. After several cocktails and attempts by other family members taking turns, it appeared to be hopeless.

"Why don't we just throw the damn urn in the ocean?" asked Will's brother-in-law. "It's heavy and will probably sink. We'll just be done with it."

That seemed like a good solution at the time, so we launched the urn with a pitch into the Pacific. At first it sank with a gurgle. As we all raised a toast to Will's memory, it stubbornly came bobbing again to the surface. We watched in alarm as it seemed headed directly to the sandy beach where families and children were picnicking and building sandcastles.

"We have to get it back," I protested. "Do you have a boat hook? Can we follow the urn and retrieve it?"

"Sorry, but I don't have a boat hook, and I can't get any closer to the shore," replied the captain.

He will probably be discovered by some young sandcastle architect and become part of the landscape," said Will's sister. "He would have liked that."

I plan to be cremated too, but I think I'll settle for a contribution to the soil of our garden.

Chapter 43
My Life Until Now

*"The way I see it, if you want the rainbow,
you gotta put up with the rain."*

–Dolly Parton

As of this writing, our daughter Anne has left her latest addiction treatment facility in Northern San Diego County. Her last few years in Tucson, couch surfing, sometimes homeless and surrounded by fellow drug users and petty criminals, could not have been happy. I pray that she one day reaches the bottom I experienced over 47 years ago. We were hoping that some of the cutting-edge work with psychedelics and ketamine in controlled clinical conditions could aid in her recovery, but she never got that far. It would be one of my happiest days to see her find a meaningful and fulfilling life, as her sister Caroline has. I also realize that the outcome is nothing I can control. I wonder if Amma at the ashram saw a dark and painful future for her.

I suppose every family has its share of pain, tragedy, and sorrow, in addition to its many blessings. Anne is ours. She was a pretty, intelligent girl who was never without a book in hand when she was young, but her path has taken her down dark and dangerous roads.

There are individuals who overcome difficult childhoods, lost opportunities or tragic events to become whole, happy and productive people. Others, raised in loving and supportive families, sometimes turn into resentful and unhappy adults. Along life's journey, we each have choices to make.

I've worked with many alcoholics and addicts since I first walked into an AA meeting. Some I have been able to help. Others chose to return to their dysfunctional lives, continuing their downward spiral. I have learned from therapy and Al-Anon that a parent is the least likely person to put an alcoholic or addict on the road to recovery.

In some ways, Anne has been an important teacher for me. I have had to face my own co-dependent issues, including my delusion that intelligence and resourcefulness could solve every problem—if I were just persistent enough. There are times when I'm at peace with Anne's absence from our family, especially when I'm with our healthy and happy grandchildren. At other times, I miss her, and her alienation is an ache deep in my heart that has no ready remedy, only occasional respite. My daughter has her own path. A parent learns to grieve, then let go.

Our daughter Caroline has worked diligently to fill the gap left by Anne's absence. She has taken every opportunity to strengthen our relationship, and I'm grateful to her for her sensitivity and kindness. I've come to cherish our time together each year at Christmas, and we talk frequently on the phone. It's a sobering thought for me to realize that she is now at the age when I married her mother, and she is now dealing successfully with her own issues with alcohol. Unfortunately, the grape never falls far from the vine.

The circle of life continues.

I plan to be the very best grandparent I can be to Olivia, Henry, and George. I encourage their interests in science and history and in visiting other countries. I would like to take them on a trip that they will always remember. Long after the material gifts are gone, it's experiences, I think, that we remember and cherish.

Gary and I have been together now for almost 30 years. It has been a good and mutually rewarding partnership of complementary, if not identical, interests. Together, we have visited 21 countries on four continents.

I have learned in AA that "self-righteousness can underlie the smallest act or thought." We often wish to hide a bad motive underneath a good one. As the physicist Richard Feynman said, "You must not fool yourself, and you are the easiest person to fool."

When we disagree, Gary and I are quick to make amends when needed. Resentments, we both understand, are like drinking poison and hoping your opponent will die. Another pearl of wisdom I've learned from AA, so much of which is counter-intuitive to our common cultural practices, but essential to a peaceful and happy life. The promises listed on pages 83–84 of the book *Alcoholics Anonymous* have come true for me and for us as a couple.

Chapter 44
What I Have Lived For

*"The whole secret of a successful life is
to find out what is one's destiny to do, and then do it."*
–Henry Ford

Perhaps every thinking person approaching the last decade—give or take—of life asks the question: "What have I lived for?" In the final months of his battle with pancreatic cancer, Apple founder Steve Jobs was purported to say, *"The wealth I have won in my life I cannot bring with me. What I can bring is only the memories precipitated by love."* According to others, his actual last words were, *"Oh wow, oh wow, oh wow!"*

I don't expect to be remembered for my education, my volunteer efforts, or my business accomplishments. I have half a dozen Lucite awards for my volunteer service that will be of no interest to the thrift store when I'm gone. The melting point of acrylic is 320 degrees Fahrenheit, so I can probably take them with me to my cremation.

One of my last searches was for the Executive Director for Funders Concerned About AIDS, a consortium of 40-member philanthropic organizations and several corporations whose support for the global AIDS epidemic continues 40 years after the first appearance of the disease. It seems a fitting bookend to my work, which started with amfAR. At least in this sector, I have made a meaningful contribution to good leadership.

For the past two years, McCormack + Kristel has been recognized in the May issue of *Forbes* as one of the top retained search firms in the country, based upon nominations by our clients and peers. It's a welcome form of recognition to close this chapter of my life.

I hope I am remembered for the times when I was the best version of myself.

In the nearly 80 years since my birth, I have lived through 14 presidential administrations. I have seen the dawn of the space age, from the Russians' launch of Sputnik in 1957 to our planning for a second moon and a possible Mars expedition in the mid-21st century. I have experienced the invention of the microwave, the personal computer, the iPhone and tablet and a computer you can wear as a watch on your wrist. The internet and social media have opened a world of knowledge—as well as misinformation. If I want an apple pie recipe, I can google it (a term unheard of before 1998), or I can join an online sect that believes three impossible things before breakfast, to paraphrase Lewis Carroll.

Few cared about pollution before the publication of Rachel Carson's *Silent Spring* in 1962. Combatting global warming has now become a priority for most national governments, though fighting the fossil fuel industry and the climate change deniers is a continuing battle, with ever increasing temperature extremes impacting our planet. It's 111 degrees in Palm Springs, our 43rd day of triple digit temperatures as I write this.

Medical science has made extraordinary progress with the understanding of the human genome. Cures for genetic diseases, as well as prevention for viral outbreaks like the AIDS and COVID pandemics are now possible because of breakthroughs in biology. We are at the dawn of the Artificial Intelligence age, with many blessings and perils ahead for us.

We have moved as a country from segregation to equal opportunity. A woman's right to choose reproduction was affirmed, then taken away, by the Supreme Court, currently stacked with ultra-conservatives. They were selected by a demagogue expressing the will of an evangelical minority. LGBTQ people, once despised and treated as criminals or mental defectives, have become an open and integrated part of society, with same sex marriage now the law of the land. Unfortunately, the transgender community, estimated to be between 0.5% and 1.6% of the population, has become the new *bête noire* in the culture wars with the political and religious right. My experience suggests that sexual orientation—and for some, gender—are not necessarily binary and may be subject to change over the course of our lives.

As we have seen with, at the time of this writing, the abolition of Roe v. Wade, social advances cannot be taken for granted. In a country of 330 million people, we have a divide between the urban, educated voters and the rural population, often limited in experience outside their local communities, and resistant to change. For every advance, there is a reaction and a sense of grievance that the voices of these rural voters are being ignored by an "elite."

With the offshoring of manufacturing jobs in the late 20th century, displaced workers challenged their anger college towards the immigrants, manipulated by wealthy business interests. As a result, we witnessed the election of a president who marshalled that resentment—the first President in U.S. history who refused to support the peaceful transition of power following an election, one who organized an insurrection to march on Congress while the results of the election were being certified. He is now the first President to be indicted four times by a Grand Jury, with additional charges possibly to come.

But again, what I've learned in AA offers solace because it encourages us to turn our lives and our illusions of control, along with our dependence on alcohol, over to the care of a Higher Power. Relinquishing control is a frightening concept for many, but it gets easier over time with experience. A Taoist would call this surrender Wu Wei, a Buddhist might describe it as letting go of the ego. A fellow AA member once characterized trust without knowing the future as a "state of grace." Whatever the description, I accept, with grace, what's to come since I'm powerless to change it.

***

I recently received a call from the Jehovah's Witnesses in Ensenada about my daughter Anne. This is a step up from the drug dealing community she lived with in Tucson. Her exasperated host was trying to put her on a Greyhound bus back to the U.S.

"Mr. Joe, we need to send Anne back to you," he said in heavily accented English.

"She can come here under one condition," I replied. "She will have to immediately go into a recovery program. Can I reimburse you for the bus ticket?"

"No, no reimburse. She must come today!"

Of course, I never heard from her after that call.

The summer of my life has passed, and the cherries have all been picked and consumed. But autumn has always been my favorite season, even before I was exposed to the glorious foliage of a New England fall. There is a bit of sweet melancholy and wistfulness as the year comes to an end, but also the promise of a new year on the horizon with the renewal of all things in the spring.

Epilogue

> *"Everything flows and nothing abides."*
> *–Heraclitus, ca. 500 B.C.E.*

I was born on December 15, 1944. President Franklin Roosevelt died on April 12, 1945, and Germany surrendered to the Allies on May 7, 1945.

During the Trump Administration, Gary and I seriously considered leaving the country. I obtained an Irish passport, which would allow us to settle in a European Union country. For now, we are remaining in our comfortable home in Palm Springs.

What are the themes running throughout my narrative? My archetypal search for my father and becoming a father—not only to my biological children, but to the many young men I've been privileged to mentor or sponsor in sobriety are important threads. So is my never-ending journey of spiritual exploration before and after joining AA. I've had a lifelong love of learning and a desire for *arete*, the pursuit of excellence as defined by the Classical Greeks.

I hope I have grown in love and compassion for all creatures. I have been blessed with the men and women and dogs who have been the companions on my journey: Rusty, Amber, Oliver, and Gracie, whose wagging tails have welcomed me home in a metronome of joy. In striving to become a gentleman, I have come to realize that the gentle part is the most important.

Patty and my sister Marianne.

I have much to be grateful for, including my husband Gary, my sister Marianne, my daughters Anne and Caroline, my ex-wife Patty, my good friends like Wayne, Rose, Stan and Billy, my fellow traveler, AA sponsor and life coach Jazzmyn—and above all—my grandchildren Olivia, Henry, and George.

I won't see the miraculous technical advances of the next 50 years, but I hope our grandchildren will. Perhaps one day they will write about their own life experience, picking the best and most important events, complete with bruises and life lessons, to leave as a legacy for their descendants, as I have attempted to do for them.

When the time comes, I hope I can say, like my mother, "I've had a good life."

# # #

About the Author

Joe McCormack retired from executive search after 45 years as a recruiter in New York and Los Angeles. For 40 years he was self-employed, initially as the co-founder of McCormack & Farrow, then as the founding partner of McCormack + Kristel, the first openly LGBTQ-owned executive search firm in the country. McCormack + Kristel opened in Los Angeles during the AIDS pandemic in 1993 to address the need by emerging volunteer HIV/AIDS organizations for professional leadership.

Before executive search, the author worked for the Young Presidents' Organization, Rockefeller Center, Inc. and American Heritage Publishing Company in New York. Trained by the Navy as a public affairs officer at the Department of Defense Information School, Joe is a graduate of the University of California, Berkeley with a degree in English.

Joe has been active on the Boards of the Palm Springs LGBTQ Center, Servicemembers Legal Defense Organization, the Point Foundation and the Gay, Lesbian and Straight Education Network (GLSEN).

Joe has had long term relationships with men and women, and he is the father of two adult daughters and the grandfather of two boys and a girl. Joe and his poet husband, who have been together for 30 years, make their home with their two dogs, Oliver and Gracie, in Palm Springs, California.